100 More Minutes with God

*1-Minute Reflections Providing
Hours of Contemplation*

By Susan Grant

ISBN: 9798797432517

Book Cover Design by Isabel Robalo - IsaDesign.net

Printed is the United States of America

Advanced Praise for *Another*

100 Minutes with God

Spiritually uplifting. These days we all need a
spiritual boost.   – Richard Clark

These daily reflections have helped to center me
on what's important as a Christian at the start of
every day.   – Zach Foster

I have Bible reading and prayer time each
morning and now your "Minutes" are a part of my
day, also. Thank you for sharing Gods' word.
       – Marian Wade

100 Minutes with God provides me
encouragement each day. This book helps build a
connection with God.   – Donna Brazell

You have NO idea how much (your minutes)
mean to me. You were used by God today.
       – Sarah Butler

Anyone can read these "minute" devotions and
get something that will stick with them for far

longer than mere minutes. Author Susan Grant has done a fantastic job with her freshman book! I can't wait for her next devotional, as well as her novel, *The Bottle House*! – NCSoccerMom

It was hard for me to believe I would get anything of substance from a one-minute devotional. But I find myself, day in and day out, truly reflecting on the words and how simple yet profound some of the ideas are. Excellent book! Excellent writing!

- Patricia Marlin

I am able to carry this book with me and pull it out of my purse when I have a free minute. This is a great book of daily devotions!   – K. Pope

I should spend more time doing devotions, but as a busy mom there isn't always time. I appreciate the short and sweet devotions that give me things to ponder thru the day.   - MJ482

Wonderful book! As a busy mom of 2, I don't get as much time as I want to spend in a devotional book... I'm able to read each section in the few moments I have in the morning, but it's enough to keep me thinking throughout the day.
- Heather Marley

I absolutely love this book! Reading through it makes you feel like it was written just for you. So many of the devotions hit home - whether it's something you've gone through or something you are going through.   – Tersa & Jason

Praise for *The Bottle House*

This book will have you reaffirming your faith along with the characters within. (*The Bottle House* touches) on several topics relevant to today's world, it will gently guide you without preaching to you.   – M. Russ

The Bottle House is a book where people make personal and spiritual connections. It made a difference in my life. Great book!!!

- Dolores A. Fox

Susan Grant has a gift. (*The Bottle House)* is a book for anyone who has a relationship with God, who is looking for a relationship with God or is caught somewhere in between.   – J.B.

The characters (in *The Bottle House*) came to life and you formed an alliance with all of them. The vivid descriptions of the pain and sorrow you felt it yourself. I highly recommend this book to anyone who wonders if God is listening.

– Rebecca Grant

Anyone who has shook their fist at God (I have), blamed God for each bad thing that's happened (I have), told God to leave them alone because they were sure He didn't care (I did). (Susan Grant) provides profound truths that can help one dealing with rejection, loss, judgement

even by those who are ministers (spiritual abuse).
A great read. Indeed, God cherishes us even when
we are sure He is silent.   – Patricia

For my dear sister, Joy Bennett. I am so proud of the woman you have become.

Acknowledgements

Many thanks to you, gentle reader. Your comments and encouragement have laid a foundation for another "100 Minutes" book. Thank you for taking the time to express to me how helpful these "minutes" have been to you.

Thank you to my husband, Randy, who has been and always will be my biggest fan and supporter. You continue to make this possible.

Foreword

We live in a world that has the most technology and innovations in all of history. What used to take hours to cover a handful of miles you can now navigate in minutes. Our lives are busy, but we still need to make time for the things that are important.

100 More Minutes with God makes it possible to connect with God each day. It offers a pattern for how to have great daily devotions. You can read each one in a minute, but its content provides you with material that you can contemplate throughout your day.

God longs to spend time with you. Why don't you join Him for a few minutes today?

Table of Contents

Minute 1

The Bondage of Fear

"All the Israelites grumbled against Moses and Aaron, and the whole assembly said to them, 'If only we had died in Egypt! Or in this wilderness! Why is the Lord bringing us to this land only to let us fall by the sword? Our wives and children will be taken as plunder. Wouldn't it be better for us to go back to Egypt?'" Numbers 14:2-3

I have battled fear my entire life. I wish I could say I'm only afraid of spiders or snakes but, honestly, very few of my fears are of this nature. Because of this, I have sometimes chosen the "known," even when it brings terrible consequences or when I know it's not the best, over the "unknown." I have probably missed out on several things that would have been a blessing and a gift because I allowed my fear to hold me back.

Knowing myself and how I tick allows me to read Numbers 13-14 with compassionate eyes. Here we have the twelve spies of Israel giving the report about what they found in the land of Canaan, the land God had promised them. Ten gave a negative report, while two gave an encouraging one. The children of Israel latch on to the report of the ten rather than the two. Perhaps it was because of their fear, and I can relate, but God is clear he was not happy with their choice, regardless of their reasons. He wanted his people to reflect on all the times he's taken care of them and then act based on this history, but their fear blinded them.

There is bondage in fear, but God's faithfulness to us through the years can shatter these chains if you let it. God's perfect love casts out all fear. (1 John 4:18)

Notes:

Minute 2

A Love that Endures

"I have loved you with an everlasting love; I have drawn you with unfailing kindness." Jeremiah 31:3

As a teacher of kids in their early teens, I have had many who say they are in love! It's often funny to watch how these kids behave and sometimes I have to work hard to not laugh out loud. They do a lot of giggling and laughing behind hands they use to disguise how they feel.

Regardless of age, love is wonderful, but with us, it doesn't always last forever. Even those in the best of marriages have to work at acting and reacting lovingly and sometimes, as outrageous as it may sound, we expect God to love as we do. I know we don't think these specific thoughts, but we can respond (or not respond) as if we believe he does.

Jeremiah tells us what God's love is like. It says it's everlasting. No conditions. No time limits. No strings attached. Just pure love. I think if we understood this better, it would transform our lives.

How can someone who knows everything there is to know about me not have his love slip a little in disappointment or exasperation? God does not love us conditionally and temporarily. In fact, he loved us before we were even born. *That's* a love that endures!

Notes:

Minute 3

I Am a Murderer

"You have heard that it was said to the people long ago, 'You shall not murder, and anyone who murders will be subject to judgment." Matthew 5:21

I am guilty of murder. It's not something I'm proud of. It's something I would love to hide, but the fact is, I am guilty of murder. But I am not the only one guilty. Jesus' words in Matthew tells us we're all murderers. No! How can that be?

If you've ever thought or felt like killing someone, you are guilty of murder. If you've ever been angry at someone, you're a murderer. After all, what is the emotion behind murder? If you destroy someone's spirit in the things you say and do, you guessed it. It's murder.

I understand these things, but it wasn't until I took the time to think through this that I saw what murder does. Murder ends someone's physical life so their bodies no longer function and the person cannot contribute to the world. Murder ends someone's spiritual life. If you cut down or despise a fellow Christian, you have hindered another's relationship with God because you have hurt their relationship with you. Murder ends someone's emotional life. In your actions and reactions, you can damage another emotionally for the rest of their lives. The list of the damage murder creates can go on and on.

It is not until you acknowledge you're sick that you'll seek medical help. When you acknowledge you are a murderer, like I am, then you can go humbly before God and ask for forgiveness and receive it. The consequences of your actions may linger for years to come, but forgiveness from God is for eternity.

Notes:

Minute 4

This Life Has Pain

"In the land of Uz there lived a man whose name was Job. This man was blameless and upright; he feared God and shunned evil." Job 1:1

There is absolutely no way to avoid the fact that in this world there *will* be pain. It doesn't matter if you are the holiest of people, pain happens. Not only that, but the more you love, the more pain you feel. Because of this, it's tempting to make your "circle of life" smaller so the hurt will be less.

If anyone knew pain and understood its damage, it was Job. Within a short time, he lost all his oxen, donkeys, sheep, camels, and his children. Then, soon after these things, Satan covered him with burning and festering sores.

Job experienced such incredible pain, but he also lived a life in the joy of knowing God will right all wrongs. This life has pain, but it also holds joy. Don't miss out on joy by trying (unsuccessfully) to avoid the pain.

Notes:

Minute 5

Law and Grace

"Because of the LORD's great love we are not consumed, for his compassions never fail." Lamentations 3:22

Have you ever noticed some Christians live only in the Old Testament–a life under "law". It could be because they feel if they live their lives according to the New Testament- a life of "grace", they would go wild, living on their terms, believing God will forgive them.

Living under the law, making sure you know every rule and you keep them is not a bad thing, but if you think you will ever be able to keep the law, you are fooling yourself.

If you think living under grace means it doesn't matter what other Christians think of the choices you've made, or worse yet, what God thinks, because you're covered by grace is fooling yourself, too.

The bottom line is, we cannot keep the law, such as the 10 Commandments and the New Testament reveals the law's purpose is to show us this. As to grace, we still have a responsibility to be an example to others, living our lives as God has outlined. It's just that grace takes the pressure off us. We do our best, with God's help, to live for him, but when we don't, grace covers us, which allows us to get back to living as we should.

It's a good thing God doesn't beat us down for our weaknesses and poor decisions. He freely gives compassion and grace.

Notes:

Minute 6

The Price of Selfishness

"The word of the LORD came to Jonah son of Amittai: 'Go to the great city of Nineveh and preach against it, because its wickedness has come up before me.' But Jonah ran away from the LORD and headed for Tarshish." Jonah 1:1-3

There are times I struggle when I read or hear the statement that people are basically good. Do I think people can do incredible, self-sacrificing things? Of course, but as I think about this, my mind always goes to the fact that we don't have to teach our children to be selfish. They know how to grab things away from others and to taunt and tease. Parents have to teach their children to share and to tell the truth. It's a hard thing.

Because we have the propensity of selfishness, the Bible is full of people who act accordingly. The book of Jonah tells the story of someone (Jonah) who did not like what God had planned for him, so he selfishly ran away. Later in the book, Jonah did not like the mercy God gave to people who repented.

In his selfishness, Jonah put sailors' lives in danger. Later, God reprimands him for his selfish attitude toward a group of people that God was going to destroy but spares because they repented.

Selfishness, something we are born with, not only affects the one who is selfish but it affects others who cross paths with him or her. This is a high price for all involved.

Notes:

Minute 7

What Is God Like?

"Who is a God like you, who pardons sin and forgives the transgression of the remnant of his inheritance? You do not stay angry forever but delight to show mercy." Micah 7:18

As a Bible teacher, students sometimes asked me, "What is God like?" You can't answer this question simply, but the Old Testament prophet, Micah, gives us some idea. He wrote God is just. He's one who draws the line in the sand and tells us, "Don't cross it." He is the very God who pardons and forgives us. Why? Because God has already had his son pay our punishment by dying on the cross for the wrong things we do. Micah's writing foreshadows this.

We also see in the seventh chapter of the prophet's book that God will not be angry with us forever; He does not hold grudges. If you have asked God to forgive you, and then ask him if he remembers the last thing you did wrong, God would say, "No!" This truth blows my mind.

Finally, Micah tells us God loves giving out mercy, not doling out the punishments we deserve. I've never met a human who can do these things, but I have a God who does. *This* is part of what God is like.

Note:

Minute 8

Faithfulness Matters

"Whoever can be trusted with very little can also be trusted with much, and whoever is dishonest with very little will also be dishonest with much." Luke 16:10

Sometimes it's good to think back on your life and focus on the big things you accomplished. When I'm feeling down, one thing I do is play through my mind a little game. I ask myself, *What would you be so totally surprised that you did in your life if you were told in your teens you would do them?* I would answer, *I never would have thought I'd teach over 36 years. I never thought I would have gone back to graduate school, while working full time and earn a Master's degree with a 4.0. I wouldn't believe I'd have a publisher offer me a book contract. I would have laughed in disbelief if*

I knew I would take voice lessons with an instructor who trains world-renown classical voice singers. As I think of these things, a smile lights up my face. I am proud of them, but sometimes I think all the little things I accomplish aren't as important.

Little things *are* important. If you leave one ingredient out of a dish you prepare, it can change the whole taste. If you don't recognize the small things you have done are really enormous things, such as your commitment to a job, your family or church, you're missing out on that blessing.

Jesus tells us in the book of Luke little things *do* matter. It takes perhaps *more* motivation and gumption to stay faithful in the small things than it does to do something "big". Jesus also taught that a good way to evaluate the character of another is to watch how they do the small, mundane things.

If you handle the small well, you will be responsible for the large. Faithfulness matters.

Notes:

Minute 9

Rain: An Equal Playing Field

"Then Peter began to speak: "I now realize how true it is that God does not show favoritism." Acts 10:34

" … that you may be children of your Father in heaven. He causes his sun to rise on the evil and the good, and sends rain on the righteous and the unrighteous." Matthew 5:45

In many households, the children growing up within those walls may have the idea that their parents and even extended family play favorites. Knowing some personalities are more compatible with a child and parent, this isn't really a surprise. As a teacher, there are some students I click with and others I don't.

That's ok as long as I don't cater to that one and give no attention to the others.

When I was younger, it was easy to conclude *God* favored some over others. When someone in the Bible cried out to God, he readily answered them and, perhaps, sent help. Sometimes I would pray about something but frowned because I "knew" God wouldn't answer me as he did those others.

The problem was, I did not understand God wants *everyone* to come to him, and he loves all equally. Maybe he communicates differently, from one person to the other, but he is always listening and concerned for all I bring to him.

God is also concerned for those who are not his children. After all, he sends the rain on the just and the unjust. We are all eligible for God's forgiveness and, in this fallen world, bad things happen to all, eventually. Despite this, God yearns for all to come to him so he can give us what we need in our day-to-day lives and in eternity.

Notes:

Minute 10

What Growing Up Means

"When I was a child, I talked like a child, I thought like a child, I reasoned like a child. When I became a man, I put the ways of childhood behind me." I Corinthians 13:11

Working with teens is an exciting thing. It brings the opportunity for me to give the gift of acceptance to them where they are and yet, I can challenge them to become the best people they can be.

One thing teens frequently say, and I did too when I was young, is they can't wait to be adults, so they can make their own decisions. They can stay up or out as late as they want. They want to decide what is best for them, but when some of these kids move into more independence; they find carrying all the responsibilities themselves is not as fun as they thought it would be.

I think this enlightenment has caused a lot of teens to continue living with their parent(s) into their 20s or even 30s because being a "child" can be easier than being an adult.

In the thirteenth chapter of 1 Corinthians, Paul addresses this issue in the spiritual sense. When I was young (spiritually) I acted like it; I reflected more on myself and my world. As I grew up, I "put away" this childish self-centeredness.

This "putting away" means to sever yourself from childish actions. It's learning that independent choices to grow up and take responsibility for what we say and do are what we all need. It is necessary so we can, or continue to be, active contributors to our families and the parts of the world where we live. Staying a child is not what God meant for us. There is a need to grow up.

Notes:

Minute 11

What Do You Harvest?

"Land that drinks in the rain often falling on it and that produces a crop useful to those for whom it is farmed receives the blessing of God. But land that produces thorns and thistles is worthless and is in danger of being cursed. In the end it will be burned." Hebrews 6:7-8

I admire those who have been farmers. I don't know a fraction of the work that is put into planting acre after acre, nurturing, harvesting, packaging, transporting and more, but I *do* know these individuals work hard.

When I drive by fields ready for harvest, I've wondered what would happen if a farmer planted seeds to grow wheat. What would they do if thistles grew instead? Most likely, they will destroy them because they know two things. The thistles are useless to them and there is a good possibility these weeds will reproduce and infect their other fields of healthy crops.

Hebrews compares this harvest of thistles to our Christian lives. If we are healthy spiritually, God can use us to feed many others. If we are living lives contrary to who we say we follow, our thistles can damage many things and people. Perhaps permanently.

It is prudent to tend to your harvest, making sure you are growing a product that is helpful and nourishing.

Notes:

Minute 12

Who Needs a Guardian Angel?

" I am with you and will watch over you wherever you go, and I will bring you back to this land. I will not leave you until I have done what I have promised you." Genesis 28:15

People throughout history have been interested in angels. If you walk through many big box stores, you will find evidence of them in books, jewelry, and cards. Owners of these stores know angels sell merchandise because they fascinate people.

Some Christians say there is evidence in the Bible that 'guardian angels' exist. It's an interesting subject, and I have read several books discussing angels' place and purposes in this lifetime. You can get all caught up on the specifics of angels, but in Genesis 28, it tells us God Himself is watching over us. There are many other places in the Bible that also record this.

God promises he will never leave us nor forsake us. (Hebrews 15:5) He knows where we are coming and going. (Psalm 121:8) God knows even the number of hairs on your head. (Luke 12:7)

Angels have a job in this life and the next, but compared to God, they are inferior. God does more than just guard us. Thank God!

Notes:

Minute 13

The Law of Cause and Effect

"Then the LORD said to Moses, 'I will rain down bread from heaven for you. The people are to go out each day and gather enough for that day. In this way I will test them and see whether they will follow my instructions.'" Exodus 16:4

The principle of cause and effect is something life teaches us in our early years, even if we don't acknowledge it. We learn, *If I do that, this will happen. If I don't do that, this will happen, etc.* This law makes things easier and less complicated. The wise person has considered the reality of cause and effect throughout their days.

In Exodus 16, we can see cause and effect in simplistic action. Isn't it interesting God operates here using the laws he made for people? He did not have to.

When the Israelites had no food (cause), they grumbled to Moses and God (effect). God heard their grumbling (cause) and provided manna and quail (effect). God gave the Israelites specific instructions (cause) and when followed; the people had plenty to eat (effect) and when they didn't; they went hungry (effect). As I think about this principle, it seems so simple. If God says to do this or that (cause), we will receive (or not receive) this or that (effect).

What seems simple in theory, however, can prove difficult. This is where having faith like a child is helpful. It's easy to make things harder than it need be. Cause and effect. Do this (or don't do this) and you will have specific results. It's that simple.

Notes:

Minute 14

Tell the Story

"On that day Deborah and Barak son of Abinoam sang this song:" Judges 5:1

I have had the honor of being taught music and voice by a professional with a myriad of credentials he rarely talks about. He would often say to me while having a lesson, "You need to tell the story" of the song we were working on. After each lesson, I would ponder the things I learned that day.

In considering the admonition, "Tell the story," I have discovered music is so important because it delivers a message or story that can engage all the senses. It's similar in the classroom. If I can find a medium that conveys the aim of my lesson, my students are much more likely to engage with the topic and carry it with them beyond my classroom.

In Judges 5, the judge Deborah tells the Israelites' story in their recent history with a song. Each verse of the chapter and song outlines how God has worked for his people, and these individuals become better people and a stronger nation because of this.

Dare to tell the story of what God has done for you–even if it can't always be in a song.

Notes:

Minute 15

In Spite of Heartache

"…Naomi was left without her two sons and her husband." Ruth 1:5

When I was young, I thought it would be a good idea to know the specific things that would happen in my life ahead of time. My reasoning was I could "plan" for it. If a gift was on the way, I could decide how to use it. If disease were just around the corner, I would work toward making it less painful by preparing my body for it in any way I could. But what about heartache? This one makes my thoughts slow down, helping me to conclude that knowing this ahead of time would make life harder.

Considering this, Ruth chapter 1 informs us that Ruth, Orpah and Naomi all deal with a heartache that will always exist in this life—

the death of someone they loved. Though we are not told the specific history of these women, we know all of them lose their husbands earlier than most. I cannot imagine what it would be like to lose my husband; my best friend. My heart aches as I think of the women, and yet, despite their heartache, Ruth marries again and her son through this union has the honor of being in the lineage of Jesus. God took something which was bad and made it into good.

We can learn to trust God through our heartaches, knowing somehow and in his time, he will make good out of them. This is hard. That's why faith is necessary.

Notes:

Minute 16

God's Economics

"So don't be afraid; you are worth more than many sparrows." Matthew 10:31

What is the value of a single human life? Many have asked this during difficult periods of history and we can see examples of this type of human economics. How about during World War II? Some humans were worth nothing; they were equivalent to trash, while others valued these same people enough to hide them from the Nazis. These types of universal historical moments are easier to identify human economics in relationship to the value of a single human life.

What can be more difficult is determining the value of "MY" life or self-economics. Jesus knew many would struggle with how much they do/don't value their own life, so he reminds us that God's economics differ from ours. He values us more than a sparrow, a creature God also cares about. He valued us enough to let his Son die for us and he would have done it even for a single human life.

Notes:

Minute 17

Good Water versus Bad Water

"My people have committed two sins: They have forsaken me, the spring of living water, and have dug their own cisterns, broken cisterns that cannot hold water." Jeremiah 2:13

If you've ever had a well dug, you know it's a bit of a gamble in several ways. First, did the drilling produce water? If so, how much water? How much money will it cost you based on how far down the digging is? There are many questions, but there is one that is very important. If your well produces water, what kind of water is it? Is the water good water, pure and sweet, or is it water contaminated with a lot of impurities?

Thinking of your life as being like a well, does it make any sense to know, through the tests of life, God is blessing your well with good water and then you refuse to drink from it? What's even more unbelievable is when you go to any place *you* choose, dig your own well, resulting in water that is dirty, and you insist on drinking that water instead.

Like a well full of pure water, God has set before us a good plan for our lives, and we can choose to drink from this well and thrive. We also can refuse it, choosing contaminated water to drink.

Why would you choose foul water when you can have good?

Notes:

Minute 18

My Statement of Faith

"See, the enemy is puffed up; his desires are not upright— but the righteous person will live by his faithfulness." Habakkuk 2:4

What is faith? Is it a feeling? Is it just a statement? Is it something you close your eyes real tight and hope for the best? Is it something that comes and goes? As you can see, faith is hard to define but, maybe it's not that complicated. Perhaps faith is acting (choosing, thinking, and doing) on what we believe to be true.

Thinking on this, I had had several events in my life recently that have forced me to evaluate my faith. I've said to God, "You say the 'just shall live by faith', but I'm struggling to do this. So, whatever you decide (in these situations), I will accept it, by faith."

Sounds like dedication, doesn't it? If I stopped there, maybe it would, but to tell the truth, I have also added to these very words, "Even though I don't feel like trusting you; even when everything within me wants to worry and problem-solve it; even when I don't think you're listening to me; I will trust." I may have to say these words over and over. God doesn't mind. I think these thoughts and feelings *are* what faith is and what we should lean on.

Notes:

Minute 19

Are You an Influencer?

"Blessed are the poor in spirit, for theirs is the kingdom of heaven." Matthew 5:3

The definition of the word influencer has changed its meaning in recent history, but the essence has always been around. These people contribute much to this world. Maybe an inventor who makes a difference to agriculture? Maybe a scientist who has found a cure? Influencer now has a different meaning, and it's often associated with fame, looks, voice or shock factors.

It's easy to think God is blessing those who have given much on this earth. I think this can be true, but sometimes we mistake wealth, power, knowledge and talent as God's sign that he is rewarding such people. Again, this can be true but, Matthew 5 tells us specific things we can do to receive God's blessing.

If we're poor in spirit; we realize we don't deserve God's blessings, but he gives them to us, anyway. If we mourn over our bad choices, we receive the blessing of forgiveness. If we are meek; we keep our mouths or actions under control. This is the blessing of true strength. If we desire righteousness; we receive the blessing of a life less complicated from our offensive actions. If we are merciful, we receive the blessing of mercy shown to us. If we seek God with a pure heart, rather than one that is selfish, we have the blessing of keeping our priorities right. And if we are peacemakers, we reap the blessing of camaraderie. Finally, if we endure the poor treatment some may give us, considering our faith, we will receive the blessing of a heavenly reward.

These types of blessings may not make you an influencer in today's society, but they are the receivers of God's praise.

Notes:

Minute 20

No Barriers

"For I am convinced that neither death nor life, neither angels nor demons, neither the present nor the future, nor any powers, neither height nor depth, nor anything else in all creation, will be able to separate us from the love of God that is in Christ Jesus our Lord." Romans 8:38-39

The school where I teach sits on a curve on a state-maintained road. Lobster fishermen are rushing to their boats, trap makers drive by, wanting to get to their jobs so they can work through their day and eventually go home. Impatient parents trying to get their kids to school also occupy this road. These factors make entering and exiting my school dangerous.

As I drive home at the end of my workday, there is another curve on this same road that is bordered by a tall hedge of dark green leaves. I always approach this area with caution because these barriers make it difficult to see what traffic is coming. I assume there is always someone coming in order to stay alert while navigating this curve. If these two dangerous areas and barriers weren't there, my drive to school and later home would be safer.

Romans 8 describes different barriers humans have. Difficulties in life, such as death, positive events, offensive actions, fears that fill us, or imbalances of power can all be like barriers or curves in the road that make up who we are. These things can sit inside us, blocking us from our connection with God. Paul's words illustrate that God has allowed these barriers and curves and welcomes anyone to come to him for safety.

Travel on because nothing can separate you from the love and protection of God.

Notes:

Minute 21

Imagination: Friend or Foe?

"Now to him who is able to do immeasurably more than all we ask or imagine, according to his power that is at work within us." Ephesians 3:20

God has given me the gift of a great imagination. Ideas for stories, lesson planning and entertainment often come easily to me. My husband has said frequently he admires how quickly I come up with ideas or how smoothly I can move from one thing to something else when the unexpected happens.

There are drawbacks to this gift, too. When I am afraid, my imagination makes it worse. When I dread something, I will always "see" in my mind how bad it will be. It is also very easy for me to assume things are not even close to what the reality of the matter is. It isn't hard for me to imagine right away the bad in situations, making it hard to distinguish whether my gift is a friend or foe.

Fortunately, God works above and beyond what I envision. I can see this when I look back over my life and spot the things God has done for me; things I never could have imagined. Limiting this life and the next with my mind would be a poor way to live. It takes faith to trust my imagination, good or bad, is inferior to what God has done, is presently doing and will do in eternity.

The bottom line is, my gift of imagination is both a friend and a foe.

Notes:

Minute 22

The Antidote
of Darkness

"While I am in the world, I am the light of the world." John 9:5

The approach of night is one of my favorite times. I love to look out my window and watch the sun go down. I must have hundreds of pictures I have taken of beautiful sunsets in every season of the year. I think it's interesting that though I love the approach of nightfall; I don't really like the darkness.

I know there are treasures the nighttime gives–beautiful starlight, a breath-taking moon and the occasional shooting star, but, for me, the darkness has a somewhat sinister effect. Living in coastal Maine, almost to the Canadian border, in winter, we will have sunsets at 3:50pm and no sunrise until after

7:00am. My hat's off to people who can live in parts of the world where the sun doesn't rise at all for many months. If we were to lose electricity on a dark and rainy day, we can feel its absence. The one thing I appreciate about darkness is it reminds me of how powerful light is, even if its source is a tiny match.

Light is vital in our lives. We need the sunlight to be healthy and to grow food. Our bodies need it to supply us with vitamin D and more. The light gives us warmth we need and, for me, it gives me the feeling of security.

The antidote to darkness is light and not the other way around. Jesus said he is the light of the world. He does not seek to impose himself on anyone and gives everyone the gift of salvation, reminding us he has conquered darkness.

Notes:

Minute 23

What's God Waiting For?

"The Lord is not slow in keeping his promise, as some understand slowness. Instead he is patient with you, not wanting anyone to perish, but everyone to come to repentance."
2 Peter 3:9

Have you ever noticed how much waiting goes on in the Bible? From the day God told Noah to build an ark until the flood arrived was 120 years. The Israelites were slaves in Egypt 430 years before God delivered them. At least forty years passed until God brought his people into the Promised Land. That was thousands of years before Jesus was born and how many years will pass before he returns in the end?

What was or is God waiting for in these examples? 2 Peter 3:9 answers this question.

God is waiting because he wants to redeem everyone; he doesn't want any to perish before they turn to him. This is good news but sometimes the waiting is hard.

I am thankful I have not been the one to dole out forgiveness and redemption. I would be nowhere close to giving the grace to others God offers to anyone who comes to him.

What's God waiting for? Could it be you?

Notes:

Minute 24

Helping God?

"Now Sarai, Abram's wife, had borne him no children. But she had an Egyptian slave named Hagar; so she said to Abram, 'The LORD has kept me from having children. Go, sleep with my slave; perhaps I can build a family through her.'" Genesis 16:1-2

"I want to help" are words a small child will say as they follow you around. As the adult, it's hard to slow down and let the child work with you. After all, if you did the task, you would be done in just a few minutes. When the child helps, it could make the task a lot longer.

What is interesting to me is when we feel they need to help *God*. This is not because we want to discover and learn like most children do when they ask this. Rather, it can be because we don't think God is working fast enough, in the right way, with the right tools and more.

In Genesis 16, many years had passed since God promised Abram his descendants would be like the stars in the heavens but, in Sarai's mind, God must have forgotten and she helps God make this happen. She gives her servant, Hagar, to Abram to have a child on Sarai's behalf.

It's easy to conclude *she's crazy! What was she thinking?* It's easy to think we wouldn't have made this choice, but we are not amid the circumstances.

Abram agrees with the plan and Hagar soon becomes pregnant. Wonderful! Finally! God is keeping his promise! Right? Wrong! The child, Ishmael, and his descendants, has brought trouble to the Israelites throughout history. This was not God's plan.

It's easy to see God directing circumstances and people in the Old Testament to fulfill his promises, but it's not so easy to trust God that he will bring to us what he wants, in his own timing. We don't need to help God keep his word. He will **always** keep it.

Notes:

Minute 25

Complaining Is Contagious

"The rabble with them began to crave other food, and again the Israelites started wailing and said, 'If only we had meat to eat! We remember the fish we ate in Egypt at no cost—also the cucumbers, melons, leeks, onions and garlic. But now we have lost our appetite; we never see anything but this manna!'" Numbers 11:4-5

I've often thought whining and complaining are similar. As I give them consideration, I think of whining as being a childish act and complaining as the adult version. Either way, it's tiresome to hear complaining.

In my teaching career, I have had several occasions when I have worked many hours and spent a good bit of money on something I'm doing with the kids and I'll hear, "Do we have to do that?" When I hear these words, several thoughts hit my mind. *How selfish you are! I'll think twice before I spend multiple hours and dollars on you again.*

Complaining is insulting and tiresome, and it is contagious, and yet we often complain to God. In Numbers 11, God's people complain about several things and he is not pleased with them. In fact, we read God's anger burned against them, literally. Even after this, they passed and we too pass our complaining on from one person to another.

Complaining is the opposite of being thankful. If we can focus on being thankful, we can break the cycle of contagious complaining. This is a choice we must make, and not something that just happens when the mood suits.

Complaining is contagious, but thankfulness defeats it. What do you have to be thankful for today?

Notes:

Minute 26

When God Asks
the Unusual

"March around the city once with all the armed men. Do this for six days. Have seven priests carry trumpets of rams' horns in front of the ark. On the seventh day, march around the city seven times, with the priests blowing the trumpets." Joshua 6:3-4

Because I am a visual learner, I imagine myself in events I read about. This often enables me to see, hear, taste, touch and even smell historical events. We can find one such experience in Joshua 6. Here you will find the record of the battle the Israelites have against Jericho.

Reflecting on the fact that God asked Joshua and his men to walk around the city of Jericho once a day for six days and then seven times on the seventh day, I've wondered what it felt like each time they walked around it. Did the Israelites think these commands were a strange thing? Were they worried about what their enemies thought? Did anyone within their hearts think, *This is ridiculous?* I cannot answer these questions because the 6th chapter of Joshua does not reveal it; I can only speculate what might have gone through my mind.

Sometimes God asks his people to do things which seem unusual on the human level. It's times like these we need to focus on what we know about God. He *is* trustworthy. He commands us to do things that are in our best interests, no matter what it feels like. It's because of these things faith is so important.

Notes:

Minute 27

Give It to God

"And she made a vow, saying, 'LORD Almighty, if you will only look on your servant's misery and remember me, and not forget your servant but give her a son, then I will give him to the LORD for all the days of his life.'" 1 Samuel 1:11

As a writer, I have always been sensitive to words and their meanings. I notice when they seem to be overused (awesome, epic, etc.). As a teacher of writing, I have frequently said to my students, "If you use the word awesome for everything- like, 'Pizza is awesome,' what will you say if you watch the sunset over the Grand Canyon? You have already diminished the word's meaning by misusing or overusing it".

Overused words weaken their meaning and I think Christians' overuse many, too, and this has sometimes been the result. An example is, "Give it to God." What, exactly, does this mean? In my literal mind, I think of trying to hold the thing we want to "give to God," lifting my arm toward the heavens, and God taking it out of my hand. Surely this is not what people mean, right?

In 1 Samuel, chapter 1, Hannah asked for a son and said if God agreed and gave her one, she would give the boy back to God; 'Give it to God'. This is more like the literal idea I had been picturing, but three things come to mind about these words. First, anything God gives us is ultimately his in the first place, so why would we think, "This is mine?" It's more like these things are on loan to us. Second, giving something to God may mean you give up your control of it. You let God show you what He wants you to do with it. Third, after doing these first two things, you let God be responsible for the outcome, assuming you have let God direct you concerning the thing/issue/person.

Is this "giving" a simple thing? No, but things that are easy aren't often worth much.

Notes:

Minute 28

Seeing is Believing. Right?

"When Joseph woke up, he did what the angel of the Lord had commanded him and took Mary home as his wife." Matthew 1:24

Having grown up in church, I am well-acquainted with the usual "Bible stories." One of them from the New Testament reveals the details of an angel visiting Joseph concerning Mary and instructing him to marry her. In listening to the story, I might think, *No wonder Joseph believed. If an angel came and visited me, I would believe, too.*

These verses tell us Joseph believed the angel's message, but what we don't know are the potential thoughts he might have had. Maybe he thought, "I must have just been dreaming. No one gets pregnant that way," or, "I must have just misunderstood the angel's message because, surely God would not want me to marry a woman who is expecting a child who is not mine." Or maybe Joseph thought, "I can't do it, everyone will think we sinned and are trying to cover it up with this story."

I don't know if Joseph thought about these things, but it certainly would have been easy for him to have had them. Either way, Joseph obeyed, by faith, and God's miracle child, Jesus, came into the world a few months later.

Believing is still a choice and an act of faith.

Notes:

Minute 29

No Calls on Hold

"Call to me and I will answer you and tell you great and unsearchable things you do not know." Jeremiah 33:3

Phone etiquette has changed so much during my lifetime. When I was very young, when the phone rang, the kids were not the ones to answer. As I grew older, my friends and I would quietly call random numbers and say stupid stuff like, "Is your refrigerator running? You'd better catch it!" and we'd hang up quickly, laughing. Today, our phone system is more complicated, and it's possible to know is calling immediately. This comes in handy if it's someone you don't wish to speak with.

Have you ever considered, however, what it would be like if God "screened" his calls, only listening to the caller who is not whining or complaining? I guess there would be a lot fewer of us talking with God.

What is amazing is God also knows who is calling him *and* Jeremiah tells us he always picks up the call. He longs to have a conversation with us about anything. Give God a call. He *will* be listening.

Notes:

Minute 30

Two Important Words:
Thank You!

"Every good and perfect gift is from above,
coming down from the Father of the heavenly
lights, who does not change like shifting
shadows." James 1:17

When I was 11, I lived in a part of the South
where orange clay was prevalent. This clay
made bicycle riding difficult. My
neighborhood friends and I would ride
around the whole housing complex and have
so much fun until we met areas of the wet,
thick clay. I can remember hopping off my
bike, taking a stick, and scraping off the mud
from around the tire's fenders. It was a mess,
but when the area dried, we could see all the
ruts we made, and we considered the mess
worth it.

There are ruts everywhere in life, too. A few come from orange clay, but most come from habits. We are so used to doing things a certain way we may not notice we are making deep impressions. If someone always rides in the middle of a dirt road when heavy rains have moved through, the ruts become more distinct, and the deeper they are, the harder it is to get out.

One such rut that comes to mind is the rut of complaining. We get into a habit of feeling like a victim, thinking everything that happens to us isn't fair and the more we complain, the deeper the rut becomes.

There is a tool, however, that will rescue us from the rut of complaining and it is recognizing all there is to be thankful for. When we focus on these good things, it moves us out of the rut and onto firmer ground.

James 1 reminds us that anything that comes our way is a gift from God and we need to be thankful. Focusing on these two important words will help us change the direction we were heading and set us free.

Notes:

Minute 31

Aging: Another Perspective

"Therefore, my dear brothers and sisters, stand firm. Let nothing move you. Always give yourselves fully to the work of the Lord, because you know that your labor in the Lord is not in vain." 1 Corinthians 15:58

There are people I have known who are/were extremely conscientious about eating right and adding plenty of exercise into their days. I always admire them because I am not as disciplined as I need to be in order to emulate them. I have seen some of these people, however, still facing deteriorating and deadly diseases. Why? Because each passing day, we grow older. Our bodies take one more step toward the grave and though we can work hard at staying fit, we cannot stop the aging process.

The opposite is true of us spiritually. With the passing of each day, we grow more like Christ–at least we're supposed to. If we are not maturing, then perhaps we need an appointment with the Great Physician, who will reveal what is stunting our growth.

Aging physically means deterioration. Aging spiritually should mean we're becoming more like our Father.

How healthy is your spiritual body?

Notes:

Minute 32

The Least Likely

"'Who are you, Lord?' Saul asked. 'I am Jesus, whom you are persecuting,'" he replied. 'Now get up and go into the city, and you will be told what you must do.'" Acts 9:5-6

When I taught high school, it was easy to notice how many teens evaluated each other. The ones who were the best looking, most athletic, and/or had the best personalities were often in the center of these teens' social world. It's interesting to see years later in each graduating class, many of the students who were average-looking, uncoordinated and shy have been the most successful in life. Spiritually, I have witnessed the same thing. Some of those I went to Bible college with, who everyone knew would be successful, have done little for the Lord.

Not only does God use for his purposes those who are the underdog, sort-of-speak, he also loves to use the least likely, like Saul of Tarsus. No spiritual leader of Saul's day was a bigger enemy of Christianity. Many of those who had turned their lives over to Jesus feared him and yet, God revealed himself to Saul and he was never the same. Saul, later called Paul, became a pillar of the New Testament church.

God loves to use the least likely for his important work. Why? Maybe so. It will be obvious they were not working on their own strength, but God was working *through* them.

Notes:

Minute 33

Be Prepared

"But in your hearts revere Christ as Lord. Always be prepared to give an answer to everyone who asks you to give the reason for the hope that you have. But do this with gentleness and respect." 1 Peter 3:15

Having spent over three decades teaching teens and preteens, I understand their brain development limitations. For example, a teenaged brain is far from being developed and the ability to predict the consequences (good and bad) of their behavior won't come for several years yet. It is also not unusual when I ask them what their opinion is about something and many cannot tell me what they think and why. If they can, their reasoning is often simplistic and non-empathetic. The times I have talked with teens about this inability to see another view, a large percentage do not or cannot see "the other side" of the issue. The kids do not understand this type of rigidity will not invite others to their point of view. Others will also be reluctant to accept and embrace biblical truths from those with such an attitude.

Considering the principles within the Bible, it's important to know what you believe and why. Saying you just feel it's true is not what Peter is referring to in chapter 3 of his first book. Not only do you need to know what you believe, but you also need to back up your principles with evidence. This is not so you can cram down someone's throat your way of thinking, but it is for credibility.

Something to keep in mind is that credibility is necessary. God and his word can stand up to scrutiny, but if you are not living your life by its principles, no one will ask you why you have the faith you claim to have. Our actions have to be aligned with our beliefs.

Notes:

Minute 34

When God Doesn't Make Sense

Then God said, "Take your son, your only son, whom you love—Isaac—and go to the region of Moriah. Sacrifice him there as a burnt offering on a mountain I will show you." Genesis 22:2

As a child, I remember thinking, *When was God's beginning?* I think back on this and other such "unfathomable" things I wondered concerning God, I have to give up. My human mind is limited and I'll never be able to understand such things this side of eternity. In Genesis 22, we find one of these types of situations where understanding God is impossible.

When God asks Abraham to sacrifice his son, Isaac, in Genesis 22, it is disturbing. Reading this narrative as a passive observer, it may be easy to conclude Abraham is a man who trusts and loves his God. I think this is a valid conclusion, but let's get into Abraham's head and heart.

Abraham was a human being with thoughts, feelings and fears. When God asked Abraham to take the promised son, Isaac, and make of him a sacrifice, Abraham's heart must have cried out, *What? You can't mean it! This makes little sense, God.* Maybe on the way to Mount Moriah, Abraham got sick to his stomach. His hands might have shaken and fear could have filled his body. The author of Genesis did not record what Abraham thought, how he felt or what he feared, so we should not assume Abraham did not experience them.

What is amazing is, as hard as it seemed, how little sense it made, how horrible it felt, Abraham prepared to do what he was told, and in the final moments of the event, God stopped him, revealing to Abraham that his faith was solid.

Even though God may ask us to do difficult things, he never asks us to do things he doesn't have a purpose for.

Notes:

Minute 35

Time Zones

"Little by little I will drive them out before you, until you have increased enough to take possession of the land." Exodus 23:30

Just as there are many time zones within the United States, people have them, too. Think of children. Their time zones are lengthy. How long the school year seems to them. What about the dark hours that must pass before they can open Christmas gifts?

Teenagers also have a different time zone than adults; theirs is short. Many want what they want and they want it now. Sometimes some continue this desire of wanting everything now into adulthood. This results in making it difficult to trust God. As we pray, we may demand God act upon our prayers immediately, but God may not choose to do this.

In Exodus 23, God has reminded Moses he will send his angel ahead of the Israelites as they prepare to move into the land God promised. Moses is specifically told in verse 30 that this process will happen little by little.

God knows when we need immediate help and when it's better for us to receive it in stages. God did this in Moses' day and he continues to do this for his children now.

Notes:

Minute 36

Your Legacy

"Now, Israel, hear the decrees and laws I am about to teach you. Follow them so that you may live and may go in and take possession of the land the LORD, the God of your ancestors, is giving you." Deuteronomy 4:1

Socrates said, "Children; they have bad manners, contempt for authority; they show disrespect for elders and love chatter in place of exercise." It's easy to be critical of the younger generation and it's interesting that many refer to them in this same manner. We believe we had nothing to do with why they act that way or hold few values.

Deuteronomy 4 illustrates why we need to pass on to younger generations what God has done in our lives. In the Israelite's day, God had protected them, fed and gave water to and encouraged them. If they would only take the time and reflect on this and pass this assurance on to the next generation, it could help them avoid some trouble.

It's important for those who come after us to see Christians flesh out what God instructs, because sometimes you are the only Bible people will read. We need to give those who come after us a legacy of living up to what we say we believe.

Notes:

Minute 37

Seeing Isn't Always Believing

"But the Egyptian magicians did the same things by their secret arts, and Pharaoh's heart became hard; he would not listen to Moses and Aaron, just as the LORD had said." Exodus 7:22

When I was a child, I often thought if I saw the miraculous things God did in the Bible, I would whole-heartedly believe everything God said or did. I even thought, *Well, no wonder so and so believed. I would too if I saw Jesus raise Lazarus from the grave* or any other miracle recorded. This thinking is faulty, however, and there is evidence of this found in Exodus 7.

When God sent the first plague on the Pharaoh, turning the water into blood, it would get my attention and most likely, the attention of others on that day. However, Pharaoh's "magicians" somehow imitated this event, and those whom God shook up over this may have wavered.

Seeing isn't always believing, and this is clear in our digital age. People and software can manipulate what we see and experience, making the impossible seem possible.

Faith is believing what God says. It is not dependent on images or imitations. Moses and the Israelites had to use this same faith during this dark period of history. Why? Because seeing isn't always believing.

Notes:

Minute 38

You Will Win but You Must Fight

"Then the LORD said to Joshua, 'Do not be afraid; do not be discouraged. Take the whole army with you, and go and attack Ai. For I have delivered into your hands the king of Ai, his people, his city and his land.'" Joshua 8:1

There are plenty of times I have thought God's help should be *his* independent work and action. I'll ask for healing, victory, courage and more, and then I'll sit back and wait for God to do these things. Sometimes God does just that, but most of the time, he is working toward a special goal or help for us, but he expects us to do our part.

In Joshua 8, God tells Joshua he will destroy Ai, but he still expected the Israelites to do the work. This is not a matter of "God helping those who help themselves"; something I think is quite narcissistic. God *will* deliver, *will* aide, *will* strengthen and many, many more things, but he often expects us to be involved.

These ideas are actually encouraging. It is humbling to me that God wants me to be involved in bringing about his will and purposes. He doesn't have to involve me, but he wants to and expects it. God has won the battle, but I still need to fight.

Notes:

Minute 39

Who Are Your Friends?

"If anyone will not welcome you or listen to your words, leave that home or town and shake the dust off your feet." Matthew 10:14

The Old Testament character of Job, who lives a life full of unbelievable events, is someone I admire. Yes, I am amazed at Job's attitude toward the difficult things he faced and his conversations with God are great examples of faith, but there is something else I admire.

Job communicated with his friends the things that were not helpful to him in his suffering. He advocates for himself. What? Isn't this selfish when we stick up for ourselves? Aren't we to be servants to one another?

The answer to these questions is, yes, advocating for ourselves *can* be selfish and it *can* interfere with being servants to others, but not always. There are plenty of ways to stick up for yourself, which are not selfish. In studying the life of Jesus, there were plenty of times he went off by himself to pray and rejuvenate (Mark 1:45). He also told his disciples they were to brush the dust off their sandals and leave when people did not welcome and believe their message.

One last thing about my respected friend, Job. We can learn from him to pick our friends carefully. Their presence in your life can make a positive and/or a negative difference. Job 4-11.

Notes:

Minute 40

What Is it Worth to You?

"The LORD your God is with you, the Mighty Warrior who saves. He will take great delight in you; in his love he will no longer rebuke you, but will rejoice over you with singing." Zephaniah   3:17

What is it worth to you to find someone who will always save you from situations, danger and from yourself, when you need it? Besides this, what is it worth to you to have someone who is always delighted to see and talk with you, no matter what you look like or what mood you're in? What is it worth to you to have this same person show his love and appreciation for you in multiple ways, always?

Would this person deserve a lump sum? A by-the-hour pay scale or more than you can calculate? Would others highly seek this person out, making them very difficult to consult? What price would you be willing to pay?

The good news is, you don't have to pay anything; God paid for it himself. His son's life for yours. Now, what is *that* worth to you?

Notes:

Minute 41

Teaching Tools

"For everything that was written in the past was written to teach us, so that through the endurance taught in the Scriptures and the encouragement they provide we might have hope." Romans 15:4

As a classroom teacher, I have found through the years that my students often learn things I have planned for them better when I wrap them in a story. These stories are often 2–3-minute descriptions of something I have experienced in life, and as I value a sense of humor, many of them make the kids laugh.

I have gleaned from this that there is much to be learned through others' experiences. The Apostle Paul reveals in Romans that much of the Bible is exactly that, a narrative teaching tool.

We can benefit from reading of lessons, often learned the hard way, of those who went before us. Check them out; they're great teaching and learning tools.

Notes:

Minute 42

Where Are Your Eyes?

"… fixing our eyes on Jesus, the pioneer and perfecter of faith. For the joy set before him he endured the cross, scorning its shame, and sat down at the right hand of the throne of God." Hebrews 12:2

I have always admired runners. When I watch them, I see a determination I wish I had. Their bodies often look toned and healthy, but running takes a lot of self-discipline. You have to commit yourself to the sport.

If you are running a race, looking back over your shoulder will slow you down or cause you to fall and keep you from the finish line.

I spend so much time looking backward; my history, my choices, and my memories. As I put one foot in front of the other, it is not helpful or encouraging to stay in the past.

Hebrews 12 tells me it works much better to stay focused on the steps I am taking now as I progress through this life, seeing Jesus at the finish line. I often have to ask myself, where are my eyes?

Notes:

Minute 43

The Art of Deflection

"The man said, 'The woman you put here with me—she gave me some fruit from the tree, and I ate it.' Then the LORD God said to the woman, 'What is this you have done?' The woman said, 'The serpent deceived me, and I ate.'" Genesis 3:12-13

Because I find words fascinating, it is not unusual that I look up the origins of some of our everyday words. The concept of blame, or better put, deflection, is an interesting word. It has a Latin origin that means *to bend* away from yourself. In deflecting, a person takes a (moral) responsibility and bends it away from him/her. In Genesis 3, both Adam *(the woman You gave me...)* and Eve *(the serpent You created....)* Try to deflect responsibility for their disobedience and they didn't fool or manipulate God.

Playing the victim in similar circumstances does not vindicate our actions; instead, it adds on more blame. Adam and Eve had no valid excuse. They knew what God told them not to do and did it, anyway. Trying to deflect the blame did not make their actions justifiable. What it did was place more distance between them and God.

Taking the responsibility for things we do wrong actually brings God and others closer because this is the first step needed for restoring the relationships we have. It brings us together, not separates. The art of deflection is a trap that destroys.

Notes:

Minute 44

Stones that Are Silent

"Yet he does not leave the guilty unpunished; he punishes the children and their children for the sin of the parents to the third and fourth generation." Exodus 34:7

We've all heard the saying that good first impressions are important. It's possible to argue about this, but we often make up our minds what we think of others in the first seconds we interact with them. Because of this, it's easy to pass judgment on anyone (including God) and on anything.

This tendency makes me wonder, if we had the power to wipe some people off the face of the earth, would we do it and, if so, how many? I err on the other extreme; I would let many off the hook; making it seem like I am a total pushover. Neither one of these extremes is good.

The wonderful thing is, *God* is the judge, not me. He can and will punish and he also will forgive. To borrow from an event during Jesus' time, the God who had the right to throw the first stone chose not to, offering forgiveness. Failing to ask for this mercy places God in the position he does not want to be in–the condemning God.

In your life, are the stones silent or are they accusatory?

Notes:

Minute 45

The Power of One Person

"But the Israelites were unfaithful in regard to the devoted things; Achan son of Karmi, the son of Zimri, the son of Zerah, of the tribe of Judah, took some of them. So the LORD's anger burned against Israel." Joshua 7:1

When you are young, it's easy to think one person cannot have a significant effect on others. After all, what can one person do? As age and wisdom permeate our minds and souls, we realize the power and potential of a single person.

A glance at history gives a plethora of examples of this, such as Mother Teresa, Martin Luther King Jr., and Billy Graham. These individuals made a positive, permanent mark on millions of people.

Just as it is a fact that individuals can leave a positive influence on society, they can leave negative ones, too. This is especially true in Joshua 7. During the preparation for the battle of Jericho in Joshua 6, God specifically tells the Israelites not to take any of the valuables of Jericho, but one individual, Achan, did it anyway. Because of this, when Joshua's army fought the city of Ai, one that should have been an easy victory, they lost and the army chased Israel as if they were cowards. When Joshua cried out to God concerning this defeat, God revealed to him the power of one person who disobeyed and brought suffering to the nation of Israel.

Yes, we all have the power to make a difference in the world. What kind of difference will you make?

Notes:

Minute 46

Lessons from the Past

"In those days Israel had no king; everyone did as they saw fit." Judges 17:6

I can't imagine a world so evil that God said He was sorry He made man (Genesis 6:5-6), but in Judges 17, we see what caused yet another biblical period of history when God's people disregarded his laws and "did what was right in their own eyes." Punishment and the consequences of these choices brought nothing but heartache to the people of that time.

If we're honest, this verse describes the world now. Many say, "No one is going to tell me what to do" and set out on a path of destruction. Even Christians can choose to travel down the same road thinking, "I know what I'm doing. I don't need to ask for God's guidance," and the same consequences are the result.

Doing "what is right in our own eyes" has a bad outcome. Perhaps we need to learn from the past.

Notes:

Minute 47

Joy Is not Situation Specific

"Yet he has not left himself without testimony: He has shown kindness by giving you rain from heaven and crops in their seasons; he provides you with plenty of food and fills your hearts with joy." Acts 14:17

Happiness can be elusive. If you ask someone what key thing they need to have a fulfilled life, many would say, *I want to be happy.* But what does being happy mean? Do you want to feel that little extra surge of endorphins throughout your day? Does it mean the events of everyday life go your way?

Pause and think about this. What would your life be like under these conditions? Do you really want to have your body hit with surge upon surge of endorphins? What character traits do not get strengthened because everything goes in your favor? I think I would rather not experience this. I would rather have joy be front and center.

Joy may or may not be an emotion. I reap it from within; when I am at peace with God, my family, and with those I work or socialize. It is the knowledge that though I do not do all things right; I am trying.

Joy is the wisdom of knowing God is at work under all my circumstances. Even the bad ones can produce something good. Joy is not situation specific.

Notes:

Minute 48

Now or Later

"Be careful not to practice your righteousness in front of others to be seen by them. If you do, you will have no reward from your Father in heaven." Matthew 6:1

We have a hard time wrapping our minds around the concept of eternity. Understanding the concept of the past, we can handle. Thinking of the present. No problem. Even thoughts of the future are workable, but when we take the future another step and try to process eternity, we don't get very far in our musings. Why? Because, except for our soul, nothing within our world will last forever.

Not only is eternity hard to process, living in a culture that has a "right now" mentality makes being patient more difficult. Picture yourself approaching checkout lines, looking for the one you hope is the shortest. Even if you think you've found it, what has it saved you? Five minutes?

We also have a different idea of what "now" and "later" means compared to what God may mean. While it's easier to think of the repercussions of our actions in the present, throughout the Bible, God reminds us that much of what we do has a greater outcome in the long run than in the short. For example, Jesus said to give now "quietly" so no one else will know and God will reward later. He also said when you pray, do it privately so you will earn a greater reward later.

God definitely has a different timetable than we have.

Notes:

Minute 49

The Illusion and Reality of Safety

"Put on the full armor of God, so that you can take your stand against the devil's schemes." Ephesians 6:11

Teaching middle school kids is both amazing and exasperating. I'm always trying to make connections with them, knowing its value.

Several years ago, I noticed many of my students had a certain name brand whose insignia looked like two alphabet letters entwined. I looked in the stores and the price tag shocked me. I couldn't believe how expensive a shirt with this logo was so, instead, I took masking tape and made the insignia on my shirt and wore it to school. Of course, the kids who wore this brand were horrified, but the others, who also could not afford it, laughed right along with me.

The brand's image was supposed to convey protection, and it got me to thinking of things that give us the illusion of safety in this life. We lock doors thieves can break through; we store weapons that may or may not protect. We make plans for action if natural disasters come into our lives. These things are good, but they give us the illusion of safety.

Paul tells us in the sixth chapter of Ephesians there is safety for God's children. The difficulty of this is God's idea of safety is often not what we think it should be. Sometimes this can mean I experience something terrifying. It can also mean bad things happen to those I love.

God can use everything, including things that terrify me, to teach me things I could not learn otherwise. Faith plays a vital role in our lives.

Notes:

Minute 50

A Little Pencil
in God's Hand

"I cannot do it," Joseph replied to Pharaoh, "but God will give Pharaoh the answer he desires." Genesis 41:16

A few years ago, my husband built me a writing station. It can hold both my computer monitors, books, pens, and paper with two small filing cabinets to hold my paperwork. Above this, I have a bulletin board and a whiteboard. As I had the joy of getting this area set up, I placed a quote above it all and it says, "I am like a little pencil in God's hand. God does the writing. The pencil has little to do with it."–Mother Teresa.

I have this posted to recognize the same thing Joseph did in Genesis 41. When the Pharaoh asked Joseph to interpret his dreams, Joseph immediately informs the most powerful (and dangerous) man in the world he could not do this but his God could. That statement must have been hard for Pharaoh to accept, as the Egyptians had many gods and they could not interpret his dreams.

Joseph knew that everything good he did was because his God helped him and we should also realize we can do nothing of spiritual significance without his help. God will help us do anything he asks of us if we let his Spirit flow through us.

It is a humbling experience to sit at my keyboard, start writing, and to see the words flow onto the screen. I can look at what I have written and marvel at what is clearly not something from my mind and fingers alone.

Joseph made it clear in Genesis 41 that he was not the one responsible for what only God could do. May we all realize we are pencils and God is the Author.

Notes:

Minute 51

Big Messes and
Little Messes

"I am the LORD, who brought you up out of
Egypt to be your God; therefore be holy,
because I am holy." Leviticus 11:45

In choosing a partner in marriage, the first
obvious thing is to see if you're compatible
in the larger things of life. Does this person
have similar goals? Are our values
compatible? What is most important to this
potential mate? These are all vital questions
couples need to answer before they make a
lifelong commitment. What I think is
interesting is if people seek to answer these
questions about their relationships to avoid
the big messes, they sometimes forget to
watch for the potential small messes. *Those*

are the ones that can cause the day-to-day squabbles.

Much of the book of Exodus is about God giving Moses, and sometimes Aaron, instructions on building the Tabernacle. In the book of Leviticus, the author describes different sacrifices and instructions given by God to these two leaders.

After reading several chapters in Leviticus, you can see God is interested in forgiving the big messes we make in life, as well as the little ones. He reminds Moses and Aaron he is the same God who led them out of Egypt; emphasizing he was in control then and he's in control now of their somewhat calmer lives afterward.

Sometimes it's easier to trust God with the bigger messes than it is with the little ones. Trust him just the same.

Notes:

Minute 52

The Gift of Music

"I will sing to the LORD, for he is highly exalted. Both horse and driver he has hurled into the sea." Exodus 15:1

I have been fortunate to have had many years of music lessons with a professional voice instructor who is also a Christian. When I watch him at work, the glow of worship and praise radiates from his face. Music/singing involves all the senses, and it is possible to sing using everything within you.

Considering this, I smile in understanding when Moses and the Israelites sing their praises in Exodus 15. They saw God parting the sea and delivering them from the Egyptians. They heard the sounds of the approaching enemies and then the whoosh of the Red Sea settling back in its bed. They could smell the scent of the waters they had just come out of. Their feet touched the land on the other side of the river, safe from their enemies, and they tasted the sweat which trickled down their faces in fear and then relief. This is when they sang their praises to God.

Music is a gift and on top of this, it will also exist in the next life. Sing something to him. He loves it!

Notes:

Minute 53

When God's
Timetable Is Frustrating

"The woman gave birth to a boy and named him Samson. He grew and the LORD blessed him." Judges 13:24

Most of us know that a day to God is like a thousand years. (2 Peter 3:8) Knowing this, it can frustrate us when we want his help now and he takes his time answering.

The Israelites experience this same frustration. In Judges 13, God's people were, once again, not following his laws and he sent the Philistines to subdue them. The children of Israel finally realize they have rebelled against God and they cry out for mercy. God intervenes, but his chosen deliverer was not even born yet. This chapter informs us Manoah's wife, conceived a baby boy, is born, grows up and **then** he, Samson, becomes Israel's deliverer.

Though God's timetable is hard to deal with, don't confuse "taking his time" with not caring or answering. God's actions (or inactions) are always for our good. We need to trust that events in our lives happen when God deems it best. Hang on through the frustration; God understands.

Notes:

Minute 54

The Problem with Assumptions

"As she kept on praying to the LORD, Eli observed her mouth. Hannah was praying in her heart, and her lips were moving but her voice was not heard. Eli thought she was drunk." I Samuel 1:12-13

It can be a very hurtful thing if someone makes an incorrect assumption about you. Take a minute and think of a time this happened. What did it feel like, and why?

In 1 Samuel 1, we find a broken-hearted woman named Hannah. She desperately wants to conceive and have a son, but this chapter tells us God had closed her womb. Her husband's other wife, Peninnah, tormented Hannah because she had children. The hurt and pain Hannah experienced both at someone else's hand and her own was almost too much to bear.

Because of this, Hannah goes to the house of the Lord to plead with God. She is so earnest she appeared to be someone perhaps speaking to themselves while drunk. The priest, Eli, saw her and assumed she was indeed drunk and chastises her for it. This assumption must have hurt Hannah and had the potential to harm her reputation.

It's easy to figure out how we feel when someone makes an incorrect assumption about us, but what about the times we do this very thing to others? Assumptions are often incorrect and can hurt many.

Notes:

Minute 55

Unconditional Forgiveness

". . . For I will forgive their wickedness and will remember their sins no more." Jeremiah 31:34

The whole idea of forgiveness used to cause me such angst. It was because I did not understand what it is, and maybe what it is not. I thought forgiveness was taking a deep breath and concentrating, trying to force myself to forget what someone did to me. No wonder I found forgiveness formidable. This idea is so far off the mark of what forgiveness really is.

You do not forgive because you have forgotten the deed. In fact, remembering makes forgiving possible. As crazy as it sounds, to make steps toward forgiveness, you need to consider what someone has done or not done to you. It is in this remembrance you can forgive. Forgiving is first acknowledging someone hurt you. Next, it is making the choice to not exact revenge, leaving it up to God to deal with.

Forgiveness is a gift God gives us and, in forgiving others, it's a gift you give to yourself.

Notes:

Minute 56

A Confused Orange

"A good tree cannot bear bad fruit, and a bad tree cannot bear good fruit. Every tree that does not bear good fruit is cut down and thrown into the fire. Thus, by their fruit you will recognize them." Matthew 7:18-20

What if an orange thought it was an apple? It could yell out "I'm an apple." It can try to get in on the apple picking industry. It can take food coloring to change its peeling appearance. It doesn't matter what it tries to do, it's still an orange. I have seen people try something similar.

There are those who attempt to cover up their bad characteristics and choices they make by presenting themselves as ones who are blameless. These individuals can fool others into trusting them.

In thinking about this, I remember Jesus spoke of a similar thing. He said others will know his children by their fruit. They can look good. They can say the right things. They can make all sorts of claims, but their fruit or their actions will quickly identify what they are really like inside.

We need to remember that if we claim to be God's children, then our actions and words have to reflect this.

Notes:

Minute 57

Love Is a Verb

"And now these three remain: faith, hope and love. But the greatest of these is love." 1 Corinthians 13:13

Some evenings, when my husband and I are sitting together reading our separate books, I marvel at how our relationship has changed over 35 years of marriage. In the beginning, love was all-encompassing. It was a time of extreme highs and sometimes extreme lows. Yes, I loved the rush of feelings the highs brought, but when the lows bombarded me, I felt its jolt.

The love my husband and I share now manifests itself in gentler ways. We are patient with each other because we know why the other reacts a specific way. We are kind and thoughtful toward each other because we know what things fill each of us with joy or stress. We are protective of each other, knowing where each of our vulnerabilities lie.

This is the love Paul speaks of in 1 Corinthians 13. Love is not meant to be a passive noun; one you receive and feel deeply. In reality, love is a verb. Verbs require action.

Notes:

Minute 58

Who Do You Turn To?

"Let us then approach God's throne of grace with confidence, so that we may receive mercy and find grace to help us in our time of need." Hebrews 4:16

Do you know anyone you would consider bold? If so, what do they do and say that makes you think this? Are they outspoken or just not afraid to speak up? Are they diligent? Do they put themselves out there, taking a risk where others may not? These things fit my idea of bold and they are qualities I wish I could have more of in my life.

The author of Hebrews admonishes us to come to God, but we can overlook the word that comes next. This word is throne.

A throne represents power and authority. I picture a child turning to a friend and asking

137

if he can come to a sleep-over that night. The friend does not have the authority to grant this request, but a parent does.

As the creator, God has the authority to do anything he wishes. This verse in Hebrews reminds us of some of these things. He has the power to give grace (giving blessings that are not deserved) and mercy (not giving punishment when they *are* deserved).

Why would we turn to anything or anyone which/who does not have the authority to grant these things? Wouldn't it be better to go to the one who can do this and more for us?

Notes:

Minute 59

In a Little While

"And the God of all grace, who called you to his eternal glory in Christ, after you have suffered a little while, will himself restore you and make you strong, firm and steadfast." 1 Peter 5:10

Christmas Eve was one of the most difficult nights in my childhood. Going to bed on this night was one thing; going to sleep was another. I remember experiencing a night that felt like it was 15 hours. As adults, time seems to pass quickly, but when you lose a loved one and you look to the future, the life you live beyond them can seem vast.

Despite how it seems to us, God repeats in his word that this life is but a "blip" on the eternity timeline. This is hard for our human minds to grasp. In fact, 1 Peter 5:10 says the suffering of this life will only last a little while. Again, there's our timeframe getting in the way.

It takes faith to trust God and keep putting one step in front of the other when the suffering strengthens. You don't have to be carefree in your heart, nor do you need to knuckle under and endure alone. God is there with you through everything and in a little while (on God's timetable), those who are his children will enter the next life; one that will have no more suffering. Hang on–for a little while.

Notes:

Minute 60

We Are Living Books

"Pharaoh said to Joseph, "Your father and your brothers have come to you, **6** and the land of Egypt is before you; settle your father and your brothers in the best part of the land. Let them live in Goshen.'" Genesis 47:5-6

I love books and my grandmother nurtured this within me. She was the librarian at her church: a badge she wore with honor. I know she would understand that when I get a new book, I will open it delicately and smell the inside binding that produces a scent that is as pleasing to me as the smell of the interior of a new car.

Books give the opportunity to live in other places, times and within other people. They have the power to teach and influence their readers, so much so that the saying, *You may be the only Bible some people will read* is important. Sometimes we can forget our day-to-day words and actions speak loudly.

Genesis 47 illustrates this when Joseph goes to the Pharaoh, the most powerful man in the world, and asks him to allow Joseph's family to live nearby. Pharaoh is quick to grant this request, even to the extent of giving Joseph's family the best land to live in. I wonder if this would have been the same result, had Joseph said things about his God and his principles and did the opposite in his actions. The answer is simple. No. None of these great things could have come Joseph's way if he had been "all talk" and no actions to back them up.

We need to remember we are all living books. What we say and do always influences others. What type of book are you?

Notes:

Minute 61

Not Knowing

"But I know that the king of Egypt will not let you go unless a mighty hand compels him. So I will stretch out my hand and strike the Egyptians with all the wonders that I will perform among them. After that, he will let you go." Exodus 3:19-20

Have you considered what effect it would have on your life if you knew ahead of time what would happen in the years to come? Would knowing these things beforehand make your life easier or more difficult? (And for this question, no cheating in your musings–it's you know everything or nothing before it happens.)

At the burning bush, God reveals to Moses what was going to happen in the land of Egypt in the coming days and immediately,

Moses came up with excuses for why he wasn't the right man for the job. God goes back and forth with Moses, who continues to make more excuses for why this is a bad idea. God reveals to Moses many specific horrible things that will happen in Egypt soon. I've wondered if God would not have revealed these dreadful prophecies if Moses hadn't insisted he was not the one for the job.

Sometimes knowing and dealing with this type of information is more difficult than not knowing it at all. Moses may have avoided the extra stress, and perhaps fear, had he immediately obeyed God's command. Knowing ahead of time most likely made things worse for Moses. Not knowing can be a blessing.

Notes:

Minute 62

In the Arms of God

"There you saw how the LORD your God carried you, as a father carries his son, all the way you went until you reached this place."
Deuteronomy 1:31

Most of us cannot remember clearly the feeling of being carried in our father's arms. Maybe for some of you, it was your mother carrying you. What's even harder to remember and face is when no one carried you.

When I'm out at the store, I'll see a father carrying his child and, most of the time, the child looks secure and happy. There's something so comforting to feel loving arms around you, protecting you from anything bad.

In Deuteronomy 1, God uses this emotional and physical picture to remind the Israelites that this is how He has protected them each step of the way from Egypt to the Promised Land, at yet they make the choice to turn away from him.

It's easy for me to understand if someone was being carried by an abusive father, they would squirm and try to get away, but these traits are not true of God. How many times have we struggled against God's arms of protection–from ourselves and others?

Dare to relax in the arms of God; He will take care of you.

Notes:

Minute 63

Our Difficulties Have
Multiple Purposes

"The LORD said to Gideon, 'You have too many men. I cannot deliver Midian into their hands, or Israel would boast against me, My own strength has saved me.'" Judges 7:2

There are so many things people say to us when we are going through tough times. "You will grow stronger because of it." "You've got this." "The pain you feel today is the strength you feel tomorrow." These aren't bad things to hear, but God often approaches our situations differently.

In Judges 7, Gideon prepares to fight the Midianites, a very strong and fearful nation. He gathers up his entire army and readies for the battle but God stops him. He tells Gideon he has too many men to fight and even explains why. He does not want Israel to think they won this war with their own power.

As this event progresses, God gets the number of soldiers down to 300. How in the world can Gideon win a battle against such a formidable enemy? That's the point. He can't.

Sometimes God gives us roadblocks that are there solely to remind us he is at work and will deliver us, not because of anything we did ourselves. This is humbling and encouraging.

Notes:

Minute 64

Foundations Matter

"Therefore everyone who hears these words of mine and puts them into practice is like a wise man who built his house on the rock.... But everyone who hears these words of mine and does not put them into practice is like a foolish man who built his house on sand. Matthew 7:24 & 26

There was a time in my growing-up years when we lived in a subdivision that constantly had new houses being constructed. As kids, we would play in them in the evenings and on the weekends, when no one was there to chase us away. I can remember looking at the progress of the houses being constructed and thinking when you have a house built, it's complicated.

I saw one house under construction years later that caught my attention, too. It was one that was built on the downward slope of a hill and when the construction crew built it; the foundation was flush with the ground. Even for someone like me who knows very little about construction, I thought it was odd to have a foundation on a house so low. In years to come, there will be constant problems of water and mud flooding into it because the foundation was not as it should be. If a crew builds on a faulty foundation, who would be interested in buying it?

In Matthew 7, Jesus said that foundations matter. He said the wise build a house on a rock foundation and the unwise build on a foundation made of sand. What is this foundation? It comprises the principles and guidelines God gives us in the Bible. Just as is true with a house, eventually it will be obvious by our actions and words what kind of foundation we have. Foundations matter.

Notes:

Minute 65

Give of Yourself Fully

"Therefore, my dear brothers and sisters, stand firm. Let nothing move you. Always give yourselves fully to the work of the Lord, because you know that your labor in the Lord is not in vain." 1 Corinthians 15:58

When we read in the Bible or other books or hear sermons on the subject, it's easy to assume what "giving of yourself fully" can mean. It must mean to always use the gifts God gave us and work to exhaustion. After all, Christians should always be busy, and laziness is a sin.

Even the Greek word for fully, περισσεύω, communicates going "above and beyond". Yet, lately, God is showing me that sometimes, "giving of myself fully" can mean I wholly admit (above and beyond) I can't do everything or specific things I deem important. Running myself into the ground is not what God meant.

The realization of these ideas can be a vital example for other believers. God knows me thoroughly; he knows I want to do what he instructs me, but he also knows when "enough is enough" and I need to rest. Perhaps God's example of graciousness is what we need to show ourselves.

Notes:

Minute 66

Spiritual Genetics

"The LORD said to her, 'Two nations are in your womb, and two peoples from within you will be separated; one people will be stronger than the other, and the older will serve the younger.'" Genesis 25:23

It is not unusual these days to do genetic testing on perspective parents. In these results, they can discover potential illnesses, health benefits, family history warnings, connections with others they did not know exist, and ethnic make-up. The problem is, these tests cannot reveal everything.

In Genesis 25, the author reveals God specifically knew about the twins Rebekah was carrying. He told her about their future nations, how they would handle family disagreements and which family will rule.

Modern testing would reveal none of these things, but the good news is, God knows our genetics and DNA, cell by cell. He is in the business of giving us the strength and courage we need, regardless of what is on the way. This does not mean pain will disappear because life in this fallen world is full of it, but it also gives us the hope that in the next world, all will be right. We don't need spiritual genetic testing.

Notes:

Minute 67

The Responsibilities of Parents

"After that whole generation had been gathered to their ancestors, another generation grew up who knew neither the LORD nor what he had done for Israel." Judges 2:10

I have taught multiple grades of children for over three and a half decades. When people find this out, they often ask me how kids have changed throughout the years. One such change I see is the digital world has saturated kids' lives, but this is far from what I notice the most. As each year passes, I see the breakdown of family units and parents shirking their responsibilities with their children.

Believe it or not, many come to school not knowing the most basic things. Many kids think it's normal to have multiple households where they bounce from place to place. Besides these things, many know nothing of the Bible and stories I heard and read about growing up: Noah and the ark, Jonah and the whale and the Life of Jesus, for example.

These spiritual things are important and we see just how much they are in Judges 2. It says here the entire generation of Israel who were alive at this point in history grew up not knowing the Lord and what he has done for their people. This is specifically because their parents did not teach them.

It is vital parents teach their kids the word of God. It may be the only place they learn of these things.

Notes:

Minute 68

Worship in Difficulties

"Moses built an altar and called it The LORD is my Banner. He said, 'Because hands were lifted up against throne of the LORD, the LORD will be at war against the Amalekites from generation to generation.'" Exodus 17:15-16

The events recorded in Exodus 17 are unusual and, as a child, I could not understand them. As long as Moses held up his hands, Joshua and his army were victorious over one of their enemies, the Amalekites. If Moses lowered them, Joshua's army lost men and a foothold. I did not understand why it was necessary for Moses to raise his hands until I read verses 15-16.

These verses reveal Moses built an altar there because he wanted everyone to remember it was in lifting his hands in worship to the throne of the Lord that God sent deliverance.

It's easy to worship and praise God when things are going well, but when we choose to worship, *despite* the difficulties and dangers, it is a pleasing sacrifice to God.

We sacrifice the desire to grumble, complain, or to question the circumstances. Doing difficult things is what makes the sacrifice so sweet.

Notes:

Minute 69

Remember?

"Now there was no water for the community, and the people gathered in opposition to Moses and Aaron." Numbers 20:2

Our memory is a funny thing. Sometimes we can remember things so vividly we can see them in our heads, feeling and even smelling some of them as if they just happened. At other times, we have no memory of events others distinctly remember. And finally, sometimes we need to just pause and reflect on specific subjects, allowing our memory to give us an advantage in the here and now.

The incident in Numbers 20 illustrates how taking the time to reflect on memories can be vital. Once again, God's people are complaining in the desert they have nothing to drink. Instead of looking back on their personal history, seeing how God supplied all their needs from Egypt until this date, they verbalize their unhappiness. God, in all of his grace and patience, once again takes care of Israel. Perhaps this will be enough to remind them God always provides what they need, when they need it.

How's your memory?

Notes:

Minute 70

Sick Pleasures

"For he does not willingly bring affliction or grief to anyone." Lamentations 3:33

There are some specific events of this life I find puzzling. When I taught high school, I could not wrap around my mind (and heart) the response of many students when they heard there was a fight. I saw crowds of kids running through the halls so they could witness it. Even within the building, I could hear students hollering, egging the fighters on. This horrified me. I could not understand why many of the students took pleasure in this.

The third chapter of Lamentations reveals God reacts, on a much larger scale, similarly to how I was feeling when I heard the heat of battling teens. He takes no pleasure in witnessing the suffering and bad choices of people. If anyone has a right to feel justification for punishing these choices, it's God, but he does not! His compassion and unfailing love prevent this.

Notes:

Minute 71

Loving Is an Act of Worship

"If you love those who love you, what reward will you get? Are not even the tax collectors doing that?: Matthew 5:46

I remember the months before my husband and I married. The feeling of joy was all-encompassing. I smile when I think about it because the love I have now for my husband is so much deeper.

People throw around the meaning of the word love and put an emphasis on a feeling that is almost in line with making it a god. Considering this, it's easy for people to make an event over a marriage proposal, but how much effort does the same couple put into sustaining their marriage?

Matthew 5:43-48 tells us love has other responsibilities. It says we are to love everyone, even our enemies.

What? Am I being asked to treat others with the same love and compassion God gives me? That can't be right. But it is. It's easy to love those we have a positive relationship with, but it's difficult to love all the others, especially your enemies. Do you see why this statement can't be referring to solely a feeling?

Considering this, I think it's appropriate to say loving in this manner is worship. We choose to love as God loves us. Treating others in a loving manner is what God asks of us, even when we don't feel like it. That's worship.

Notes:

Minute 72

Grace Is Better

"Clearly no one who relies on the law is justified before God, because "the righteous will live by faith." Galatians 3:11

In a lot of ways, rules work for me. Life taught me what the rules are and I do my best to keep them. I have rules for work, rules in the classroom, rules on how to interact with others and rules for myself. Having these allows me to measure how well I am doing here on earth and if I'm living the life God meant for me spiritually.

The best biblical example of rules is the 10 Commandments. If I go right down the list of what I should and shouldn't do, I can measure how well I am doing spiritually. The problem with this is I can never keep all the rules, all the time, and unless I change my spiritual focus, when I compare my actions to God's rules, I will always be inadequate.

Fortunately, Jesus, who kept all the rules, died in my place. Now, I don't need to spend all my energy worried because I cannot live up to the standards of God's rules. Paul tells us in the book of Galatians that we need faith to live by grace; grace being that God will not condemn me for not keeping the rules.

It's hard to trust that Jesus' death is all I need. I sometimes think if I live by grace only, then I'll "run wild" sort-of-speak and do whatever I want. But this is not how a child would want to be when he or she is being raised by a loving God.

What I do for God, out of gratitude, is not the same as striving to keep rules I cannot keep. Grace is better.

Notes:

Minute 73

Satan Believes in God

"You believe that there is one God. Good! Even the demons believe that—and shudder." James 2:19

Holidays now differ from the ones I had as a child. No, the dates and titles for most of these days have not changed, but their emphasis has.

Christmas used to be solely about Mary and Joseph going to Bethlehem to be taxed and while there, the Savior, Jesus, was born. Now, many focus the celebration on Santa and on a general sense of goodwill among people. Easter used to be an acknowledgement of Jesus being crucified on the cross for our sins and then his resurrection. Now, we have Easter bunnies and egg hunts.

Both days, for many, have lost the element of faith and the worship of God. It's almost as if it's not all right to believe in God anymore. This is sad and ironic. Why? Because Satan and his demons believe in God.

James tells us the Evil One and his demons know there is a God and they are afraid of him. That's more recognition than many today show God, but Satan's belief is only an acknowledgment; he does not seek God's forgiveness and a relationship with him.

If all we have in our spiritual life is solely a belief that there is a God, it's not the same as being his child. You can become his child if you ask for forgiveness, accept his salvation, and then live according to his principles. This alone will change the emphasis on Christmas and Easter.

Satan will never be a child of God; he will not be in heaven for eternity. Will you?

Notes:

Minute 74

Watch!

"Be alert and of sober mind. Your enemy the devil prowls around like a roaring lion looking for someone to devour." 1 Peter 5:8

Living on the coast of Maine, away from the bigger populations of the southern part of the state, there are few cities. We have no traffic lights–unless you count one that is only a flashing yellow light. To go to a big-box store, you must travel at least 50 miles. Because we are in such a rural area, when I walk, I need to consider the fact there are wild animals around; therefore, I carry pepper spray just in case.

Most of the wildlife here is not dangerous, but one time on a walk, I encountered a black bear, eating blueberries. I remember it stood up and my heart skipped a few beats. I backed away slowly, and fortunately; it did not follow. From that point on, I look around regularly while walking and it reminds me I need to do the same thing spiritually.

1 Peter 5 tells us we need to be vigilant in watching because Satan is like a lion, waiting to destroy us. Peter does not say to let this information paralyze us in fear; instead, he tells us to be watching. A lion and other animals of prey often attack from the place of secrecy so they can successfully kill their prey. Watch!

Notes:

Minute 75

Not "I Promise" but "I Will"

"When Abram was ninety-nine years old, the LORD appeared to him and said, 'I am God Almighty; walk before me faithfully and be blameless. Then I will make my covenant between me and you and will greatly increase your numbers.'" Genesis 17:1

A while ago, my husband had a serious illness which resulted in a hospital stay. It really shook me up and even after the doctors released him and his symptoms were mostly gone, I would say to him, "I know what your answer is going to be, but I need to ask it. Are you OK?" What I needed was reassurance and in receiving it, I could relax, at least for a time.

During the emotional upheaval during his illness, I noticed something in Genesis 17. In the New International Version of the Bible, God uses "will" 31 times. As I read through this passage, I also noticed God did not use "promise". Why? I'm not a Hebrew scholar, but my understanding of the word promise is that it gives reassurance about something. Instead, God told Abraham he **will do** several things.

God's word is not dependent on whether we believe and/or need reassurance. God *always* keeps his word and, sometimes, he gives extra reassurance to his people, not because he needs to validate what he says, but because he knows we need it.

Notes:

Minute 76

Laws We Cannot Keep

"You shall have no other gods before me."
Exodus 20:3

Life is often difficult. Circumstances may place demands on us we know immediately we cannot meet. What if those in authority over us gave us some specific demands and informed us that the repercussions of not meeting them are death? Our response might be to rebel, to ignore, to hide, or to confront the one who is demanding.

If all the 10 Commandments found in Exodus 20 exist to be enforced today, many would react in the same way. Yes, these commandments are there to inform us of boundaries and choices God gave us and, yes, the punishment for not keeping them is death. How is this fair that God knows we cannot keep these laws and yet expects we keep them? This seems cruel.

Those who are not God's children may use these specific ideas to reject Christianity, and it's understandable on a certain level. However, these laws exist to show us no matter how hard we try, we *cannot* keep them.

Are we doomed? No! There is One, Jesus, who was born in Bethlehem, who kept these laws and yet, he willingly let the leaders of his day put him to death and he rose again on the third day. The amazing thing is God will accept Jesus' death in place of ours. We only need to ask. This is grace; the law cannot give it.

Notes:

Minute 77

Biting Circumstances

"The LORD said to Moses, 'Make a snake and put it up on a pole; anyone who is bitten can look at it and live.'" Numbers 21:8

I heard someone say once, "No one ever gets away with anything." and my first reaction was, "That's not true." Since then, I have been thinking about this and I've concluded his statement is correct. There are always consequences attached to the bad choices we make. Some may come as a punishment, a breakdown in a relationship, hurt feelings, and multiple other troubles.

In Numbers 21, we see a deadly consequence for the children of Israel, who are still moaning and complaining about their circumstances. We read here God was not happy with their complaining, so He sent poisonous snakes that bit many of them and they died. It was then the people came to Moses saying they were sorry for their words and actions and there are two interesting things God does or doesn't do that are worth noting.

God **gives** Moses instructions to make a bronze snake and put it on a pole. If anyone looked at this snake, God healed them. What God **does not** do is take away the snakes.

My thinking about this is we have to live with the consequences of what we do (or don't do), even when God forgives and heals. Wouldn't it be better if we just do what God wants us to do?

Notes:

Minute 78

Young Love and Old Wisdom

"Some time later, he fell in love with a woman in the Valley of Sorek whose name was Delilah." Judges 16:4

Sometimes while I'm driving, I hear a song which places me in a mental time machine and before I know it; I am 35 or more years in the past. If I take the time to relive a specific moment, I smile and then cringe. My naivete screams when I remember what I thought was a potential love that would last a lifetime. I realize some people have the fortunate circumstances of finding the love of their life early and are still going strong, but in my case, that would not have been the outcome. In consideration of this, there have been many times I have thanked God for *not* giving me what I asked for. Today, in my late 50s, I have the wisdom to see what is lasting and what is merely an emotional reaction.

In Judges 16, Samson makes the mistake of youth; he falls for a woman named Delilah. He does not have the wisdom of thinking this relationship through, nor does he seek wise counsel from others. What he thought was true love and a good decision turned out to be his downfall.

There is nothing wrong with young love, but the wisdom gained through the years knows sometimes a person is running *from* something rather than *to* someone. If Samson had considered this, perhaps he would have had a longer life.

Notes:

Minute 79

A Student of History

"You alone are the LORD. You made the heavens, even the highest heavens, and all their starry host, the earth and all that is on it, the seas and all that is in them. You give life to everything, and the multitudes of heaven worship you." Nehemiah 9:6

Sometimes, when I get discouraged, I take the time and review my history, specifically concerning what the Lord has done for me. I have done this in several ways. Sometimes I just start out counting my blessings–which there are a lot of. Another thing I do is think of what God has helped me accomplish. This, too, fills my heart with gratitude.

In Nehemiah 9, we see an example of the author reviewing his nation's history. Nehemiah records, in part: creation (vs. 6): blessings of his people (vs. 7-8); freeing the

Israelites from the slavery of Egypt (vs. 9-12); rules to live by (vs. 13-14); provisions of food and water when needed (vs. 15); and recognizing God stayed with his people despite their disobedience in the desert (vs.19-21).

If we take the time to review what God has done for us through the years, it will be a source of comfort and strength when we need it most. Be a student of history.

Notes:

Minute 80

Rest Is Underrated

"Take my yoke upon you and learn from me, for I am gentle and humble in heart, and you will find rest for your souls." Matthew 11:29

One year, I had to accompany a group of 8th graders on a trip to Boston. (Sounds fun, doesn't it? I guess your answer really depends on your age–at least it's that way for me.) We left the school at 4:30 am and returned at 3:30 am the next day. I guess I was the lucky teacher because I got assigned the 4 rowdiest boys to chaperone. This was the first–and only time, I hope, when I had no sleep in a 24-hour period.

When we finally arrived back at school, I remember driving the short distance home at 25 mph just because I really couldn't see straight. My mind was slow in thought and the rest of me followed suit. It was my body's way of telling me, "You need some sleep!"

I think this memory is an excellent illustration of why we need rest in our spiritual lives, too. Jesus promised his children rest. When your spirit is not at rest with God, it can be just as dangerous as it was for me to drive home that morning.

Without spiritual rest, it's easier to make poor critical decisions, to say things you wish you hadn't, and to not listen and hear what God has to say.

Jesus said he delights in giving his children rest. Rest. Calm. Peace. Rest is underrated.

Notes:

Minute 81

Keep Looking

"Consider it pure joy, my brothers and sisters,[a] whenever you face trials of many kinds." James 1:2

As a child progresses from walking to talking, there is one question he or she asks so frequently it can be annoying. This question is, why? *Why does a dog bark? Why is that woman so loud? Why can't I stay up later?* These sorts of questions may drive adults crazy, but if we're honest, we discover we ask many "why" questions, too.

One of the hardest facts of life we must deal with is that difficulties are a part of living. Some difficulties are harder than others. It's easy for this to side-swipe us because when it does, we may say to ourselves, why me? In my mind, I think if I can just understand the whys of life, I can cope.

Eventually, everyone will walk down the path of difficulties, which include arguments, tragedies, betrayals, disease, depression, and death, and when we ask why, there is no immediate answer. A favorite quote illustrates this friction well. Jane Kirkpatrick wrote, "Some things are forever left to chewing without the satisfaction of a swallow."

If we keep this in mind, we can readjust our focus. Some difficulties in life will only leave us chewing. We can then choose to accept, by faith, that these difficulties will work for our good. God always takes the problems of this life and uses them to make us better. Keep looking for the good; it is not hiding.

Notes:

Minute 82

Hatred Is Powerful

"So Joseph went after his brothers and found them near Dothan. But they saw him in the distance, and before he reached them, they plotted to kill him." Genesis 37:17-18

Hatred is powerful. It can motivate, burn, rage and murder and where it is present, it affects all people involved and not positively. There have been psychological studies of the effect of hating someone, but you really don't need to read these. All you have to do is observe what hatred does to people.

In Genesis 37, Joseph's brothers hate him so much; they begin a series of actions that change the course of all the lives of those involved and their future families as well. The brothers rage in hatred and isolate Joseph. They sell him for a little money and then forge a series of lies they tell their father, hoping to cover their tracks.

Yes, God uses even these horrid things for his good in Joseph's life, but even this did not make the hurt and pain leave Joseph. These events left their mark upon his soul. Hatred is an evil thing.

In the Sermon on the Mount, (Matthew 5-7) Jesus said hating someone is the same as murder. We would be wise to run from it when we notice the first traces of it in our lives. Why? Because hatred is so powerful, the feeling alone can cause significant damage.

Notes:

Minute 83

Fear Examined

"When the Egyptians see you, they will say, 'This is his wife.' Then they will kill me but will let you live. Say you are my sister, so that I will be treated well for your sake and my life will be spared because of you." Genesis 12:12-13

Fear can be a useful thing. It can prevent us from driving too fast or from throwing gasoline on a fire. It alerts us to things in life we should treat with caution. Fear can be debilitating, too. Doctors can trace many illnesses, including ones that are physical, mental and emotional back to it. Fear can cause someone to make certain decisions they would not have made otherwise.

In Genesis 12, we see a side of Abram that is not revealed earlier. In the chapter, he and his family travel to Egypt because of a famine and he thinks because he has a beautiful wife, his life would be in danger there. In his irrational fear, and I use the word irrational because God had already promised him and his family Canaan, he pressures his wife, Sarai, to claim Abram was her brother because he feared for his life. This lie allows the Pharaoh to take Sarai and make her a "wife" and all this implies. I have wondered how Sarai felt about this. Because her husband feared for his life, she was "left" with the Pharaoh. Fortunately for Sarai, God intervened and gave her back to Abram, leaving Pharaoh bitter about all of this. Pharaoh then banishes Abram from the land.

Fear is a powerful thing and can make it easier for poor choices to be made. Fearing the circumstances of everyday life is not from God because 1 John 4:18 reminds us that "perfect love (the love God gives us) casts away all fear." Love trumps fear; rest in God's love.

Notes:

Minute 84

Admitting We Are Wrong

"So now, if the boy is not with us when I go back to your servant my father, and if my father, whose life is closely bound up with the boy's life, sees that the boy isn't there, he will die. Your servants will bring the gray head of our father down to the grave in sorrow." Genesis 44:30-31

Admitting I am wrong is sometimes a struggle. It's not because I don't want to "own" my poor judgment, word or action; it's because I'm afraid if I bring to others' attention my error, then they would have nothing to do with me. Sometimes I think there's not much worth cherishing within me. There are many reasons this is wrong thinking, but one of them I see in Genesis 44 and in my life as well.

Joseph, the now 2nd in command in Egypt, tests his brothers to see if they could admit their bad choices of how they treated him in the past. In Genesis, we see Judah, representing the rest of his family, is truly sorry for his past actions and realizes now the affect they had on his father. The brothers learned from and admitted their bad choices.

One of the most beautiful things someone did for me is when, in tears, I told her about an event that put me in a face-to-face talk with my bosses. She smiled and told me of a time when she had to face the same thing. It was such a blessing and relief to hear her words, reminding me I am not alone.

I realized admitting I am wrong–not just to those involved but also, when appropriate, to others whose situation could benefit from hearing can make a vast difference in another's life. God can use these things to free others whose circumstances have bound them in these same chains.

This is beautiful. Admit it!

Notes:

Minute 85

The Formula for Compassion

"The LORD, the LORD, the compassionate and gracious God, slow to anger, abounding in love and faithfulness, maintaining love to thousands, and forgiving wickedness, rebellion and sin. Yet he does not leave the guilty unpunished." Exodus 34:6-7

When I hear or read the word compassion, it soothes my soul. It's like my entire body has been tense–ready to run, fight or hide and then I hear compassion and I automatically relax my muscles.

What is it about compassion that can cause this blessed reaction? It is in discovering the meaning of the word found in Exodus 34. Compassion in the Hebrew language comprises two things: mercy and forgiveness. These meanings portray a characteristic of a God who has great healing.

If you grew up thinking God is solely a judge, ready to dish out punishments, it's not a balanced understanding (on the limited level of understanding humans have concerning God.)

This chapter of Exodus reads God is compassionate; He gives mercy, not giving out a punishment we deserve, and forgiveness similar to a pardon.

Mercy and forgiveness make up the formula of compassion. Dare to embrace this.

Notes:

Minute 86

Your Reputation Has a Long Shadow

"'We have heard how the LORD dried up the water of the Red Sea[a] for you when you came out of Egypt, and what you did to Sihon and Og, the two kings of the Amorites east of the Jordan, whom you completely destroyed.'" Joshua 2:10

As a teacher of middle school kids, my students fluctuate between caring way too much about their reputations and not caring at all. As they grow older, many realize, sometimes the hard way, the value of having a trust-worthy reputation. They will lament to me, "My parents will never trust me again." This is a consequence of not valuing your reputation enough.

In Joshua 2:8-11, the people of Jericho know of the Israelites' and their God's reputation. This knowledge gives the children of Israel an advantage as they move into the Promised Land. It is, ultimately, what tips the scales in Israel's favor.

Pondering this, I've wondered how this period of history would have gone if God's people had a poor reputation. This, too, casts a long shadow.

In consideration of this tendency, it would be prudent to examine your reputation, though not controlled by it. A good reputation holds a lot of weight, but so does a bad one.

Notes:

Minute 87

The Importance of a Semi-Colon

"So we say with confidence, 'The Lord is my helper; I will not be afraid. What can mere mortals do to me?'" Hebrews 13:6

It was fortunate my parents drilled into me many grammar rules. For example, I can remember my father telling me when you answer the phone and someone asks to speak to Susan, proper grammar dictates my reply should be, "This is she." Yet, even though I had this practical training, there were many such rules I picked up while teaching.

I did not start out as an English teacher; therefore, I learned a lot of grammar as I instructed my students. One of these many lessons involves the semi-colon. It is an under-used punctuation. You use semi-colons when you have two independent clauses that are virtually cause and effect. For example, I am tired tonight; I will not go to the game. Why do I not go to the game? Because I'm tired.

Hebrews 13 includes a quote from the Psalms and it uses a semi-colon. "The Lord is my helper; I will not be afraid." Why will I not be afraid? Because the Lord is my helper. Focusing on why I shouldn't be afraid, God will help me, reminds me I am not alone.

Though circumstances in this life can be difficult, I am not alone and help is available. A semi-colon is important.

Notes:

Minute 88

God Loves, When We Don't Deserve It

"So Pharaoh said to Joseph, 'I hereby put you in charge of the whole land of Egypt.' Then Pharaoh took his signet ring from his finger and put it on Joseph's finger. He dressed him in robes of fine linen and put a gold chain around his neck. He had him ride in a chariot as his second-in-command, and people shouted before him, 'Make way[!]' Thus he put him in charge of the whole land of Egypt." Genesis 41:41-43

The life of Joseph, as recorded in Genesis 41-50, is my all-time favorite one to study except for the life of Jesus. I've even named my protagonist, Joseph, in my novel, *The Bottle House*, in honor of Jacob's favorite son.

I admire so much of Joseph's character. If anyone had a right to be bitter and angry, Joseph did. His brothers bullied, lied about, and sold him as a slave, and then his overseer's wife accuses him of rape. Despite these, Joseph stayed true to his God, thus bringing much-needed food to the known world for seven long years of severe drought.

As I think about these events, I realize that in supplying food during this bleak time, God was providing for the needs of the very people who mistreated Joseph and to nations of people who did not accept him as God. What an example of unconditional love.

God did not stand there, cross his arms and say, "Yes, these people will receive this nourishment and those people don't." Jesus told us himself that God sends the rain on the just and the unjust. (Matthew 5:45) This is the love that made it possible for Joseph to endure so many difficult things, and if we allow it, love can make it possible for us, too.

Notes:

Minute 89

Human Nature

"That same day Pharaoh gave this order to the slave drivers and overseers in charge of the people. 'You are no longer to supply the people with straw for making bricks; let them go and gather their own straw. But require them to make the same number of bricks as before; don't reduce the quota.'" Exodus 5:6-8

One of the good things about life is we cannot control other people and one of the difficult things of life is we cannot control people. It's easy to sit back and not worry about others when they are treating you well, but what about when they choose to treat you poorly? In these circumstances, the temptation might be to shut them down in what they say and do. Using energy in attempts to do this very thing is a waste of time. The only thing we *can* do is control how we *react* to what others say and do.

In Exodus 4, Moses obeyed and told Pharaoh God said to let his people go. Pharaoh's response was quick and severe, ordering the Hebrew slaves to do more work and still produce the same number of bricks for his many projects.

Thinking about this from a slave's perspective, I would probably get angry at Moses, the Pharaoh and God. I might even try to come up with some ways to manipulate those involved, so this outrage might end.

This attempted manipulation would be a total waste of energy. The Pharaoh's actions and words were his own and no one could change them. What the Israelites *could* control is their reaction to what Moses told them concerning God delivering them from slavery. This doesn't mean they liked what was happening to them.

It seems it's in our nature to control others, but this will never bring productive results or bring about the change we wanted.

Notes:

Minute 90

Are You a Skeptic?

"Keep his decrees and commands, which I am giving you today, so that it may go well with you and your children after you and that you may live long in the land the LORD your God gives you for all time." Deuteronomy 4:40

If you have heard that a person should not question God either in words or actions, perhaps it's time to reevaluate this. I don't think it's wrong to bring up these types of things with God. A lot depends on your motivation.

For example, I tell my students if they question me about something I have told or did to them, they can come to me with these things. I then tell them what's really important is *how* they ask me. I then follow up and tell them when they learn to trust me, the less they will feel they need to do this.

In Deuteronomy 4, God is telling his people something similar. He tells them to keep his commands and the result will be a life that has less conflict and distress. I also see an underlining "permission" to test God's words. Live a life based upon God's blueprint for our lives and see if we have a better one.

Does this mean all of our lives are going to be wonderful? No. What it means is, no matter what comes our way, if we choose to do what we know is right, in the long run, it will cause us fewer problems and we can thank God for recognizing this in our lives.

Are you a skeptic? Try out the words of Deuteronomy 4 and see for yourself if your life is better for it.

Notes:

Minute 91

The Difference Between Hope and Faith

"Now faith is confidence in what we hope for and assurance about what we do not see." Hebrews 11:1

Hope is powerful. It is the strength I have read about in many holocaust survivors' memoirs. It is the foundation of those who are dealing with debilitating diseases. It lingers in the hearts of parents when they see their children making poor choices. Though hope is vital, it is not the same as faith.

It's easy to confuse "hoping for" with "faith". I hope God's promises are true versus, I believe, they are. If we think God's promises are only "hopefuls", making plans and life-decisions based on this foundation would be imprudent.

If we know God keeps his word because we've seen him at work in the Bible and in our lives, we can decide and make choices based on faith.

Faith is not a feeling either. Feelings are reactions to circumstances. Faith is a verb. You make the choice to take God at his word and act upon it.

Notes:

Minute 92

Taking the High Road
Isn't Easy

"The midwives, however, feared God and did not do what the king of Egypt had told them to do; they let the boys live." Exodus 1:17

Sometimes in this life, when circumstances, illness, stress, and strained family relationships become unbearable, it can cause many to act in contradiction to their values. It's also possible, though difficult, for someone to make a stand when the push of society is toward living a life contrary to God's laws and principles. This taking of the high road sounds admirable, but this nobility is costly.

In Exodus 1, the Israelites, who are now slaves, are becoming a threat to Egypt's Pharaoh. He orders their work increased and, ultimately, the death of any baby boys. During this unimaginable time, there were those who took the high road and refused to obey the king. This placed their lives in the Pharaoh's hands and yet, a baby boy is born and the Pharaoh's daughter brings him up to live in the very palace the authorizer of this mass killing lives.

God honors taking the high road. You may not realize it in this world, but how beautiful are the examples of those who *dared* to walk this path.

Notes:

Minute 93

When Trust Is Difficult

"When they came to Marah, they could not drink its water because it was bitter. (That is why the place is called Marah.]) So the people grumbled against Moses, saying, 'What are we to drink?'"" Exodus 15:23-24

When you trust someone, you have a calm within. This is because you know this person will keep his or her word; they are dependable and they accept you for who you are–flaws included. When trust becomes difficult is when your circumstances put you in the center of chaos, exhaustion, doubt, and more. Trusting under these circumstances really is more about you than the object of your trust. They scare you. They hurt you. They tire you out. These things make trusting difficult and, in these moments, it's hard to reflect on what you know about the object of your trust.

Near the end of the fifteenth chapter of Exodus, we see the Israelites in the Desert of Shur. They are hot, tired, cranky and afraid. At least they knew they had the food and water they needed when they were slaves, and now, they weren't sure if God would take care of their needs.

When the difficulties of life blind you to the history of the faithfulness God has had toward you, it's hard to trust him. It becomes necessary to see beyond these things and think; *I know what it feels like. I know what I see. I know my body is crying out for what it needs. Yet, even now, I choose to trust.* It may be only words you say to God, maybe with fear and confusion, and yet, this is the first act of trust. The other steps will follow.

Dare to trust; even when it's difficult.

Notes:

Minute 94

Resentment Unleashed

"'Isn't it enough that you have brought us up out of a land flowing with milk and honey to kill us in the wilderness? And now you also want to lord it over us!'" Numbers 16:13

Resentment forms when you have the idea others have treated you unfairly. You become the judge and you evaluate situations, determining which ones have treated you fairly and which haven't. What can become a real problem with this evaluation is you rarely have all the facts, and it's therefore easy to jump to conclusions you should have factored into the situation.

I have found myself in similar circumstances. I am treated a specific way; I make an erroneous conclusion and therefore resent the people involved. Resentment does not make the situation better, and it takes its toll on us physically, emotionally, and spiritually.

In Numbers 16, we find a man named Korah who resents Moses and the circumstances he finds himself in. He groups up with others who have similar resentments and they bring their complaints to Moses and, ultimately, God.

God is not pleased with this and through Moses, He figuratively draws a line in the sand. That day, God opens the ground and Korah and his followers fall in and God closes it just as fast. This is a testament to all that resentment is not a good thing and can lead to difficulties and sometimes death.

Is resentment killing you?

Notes:

Minute 95

Deception Is Never a Good Thing

"Rebekah said to her son Jacob, 'Look, I overheard your father say to your brother Esau. Bring me some game and prepare me some tasty food to eat, so that I may give you my blessing in the presence of the LORD before I die. Now, my son, listen carefully and do what I tell you.'" Genesis 27:6-7

I have a quote book where, for many years, I have written things I want to remember. One such quote is, *A liar better have an excellent memory.*

Deception is becoming a common thing in society. In fact, our specific words for lying attempt to play down its moral implications. Lying is now referred to as a fib, a falsehood, and a little white lie. It really doesn't matter how you dress it up, a lie is a lie and deception is never a good choice. Yes, there can be arguments that telling the whole truth isn't always kind, but deception is a bad thing, a sin.

In Genesis 27, Jacob, with the help of his mother, Rebekah, deceived Isaac and steals the birthright and blessing, all the rights of the family property and more from his twin brother Esau. Yes, Jacob was successful in his deception in the material sense, but he paid for it. He was constantly on the run because Esau vowed to kill him. He has very few moments of rest in the years to come.

Deception is never a good thing.

Notes:

Minute 96

Trash Talking

"'But this is not true of my servant Moses; he is faithful in all my house. With him I speak face to face, clearly and not in riddles; he sees the form of the LORD. Why then were you not afraid
to speak against my servant Moses?'"
Numbers 12:7-8

It certainly is human to trash talk someone. Why not? Our culture has saturated itself with it. It's on the news, in entertainment, at the local grocery store and even in churches.

In Numbers 12, we see how God feels about trash talking. Moses' siblings, Miriam and Aaron, don't care for some things Moses, as God's representative, does. They stir God's anger, and he strikes Miriam with leprosy and, even though Moses begs God to heal her,

God kept her away from the Israelites for seven days.

Perhaps God isolated Miriam to keep her trash talking opinions from spreading among the people. That's one problem with this talk.

Let's take out the garbage today and save our words for encouragement.

Notes:

Minute 97

God's Navigation

"When Pharaoh let the people go, God did not lead them on the road through the Philistine country, though that was shorter. For God said, 'If they face war, they might change their minds and return to Egypt.' So God led the people around by the desert road toward the Red Sea." Exodus 13:17-18

What we see is far from all there is. I had a professor in college who told us the human eye only sees 1/10 of 1% of what there is to see. For example, we do not see germs, cells, and oxygen. The human eye also cannot see the spirit world, such as angels and demons. It will truly be an experience to see some of these and much, much more in the next life. Because our sight is limited, we also do not see the things God does and when he leads us in certain directions, we may think it makes no sense. We need to trust him.

In Exodus 13-14, we read of God's thoughts on where to lead the Israelites after they leave Egypt. He wants to bring them to Canaan, but he knows his people will be overwhelmed if they have to go to battle with the Philistines. Therefore, God leads them toward the Red Sea. This change of route may have felt good at first: no war with the Philistines, but the shore of the Red Sea traps the Israelites and Pharaoh and his men are coming towards them. How frightening and confusing this must have been for God's people. They must make the choice to reflect on what God has done to get them delivered from slavery and then they can conclude God knows what he's doing. I know, easier said than done, but God *delivers* them.

God's navigations are always the best direction for us. It may not feel and seem like it, but we don't see everything there is to see.

Notes:

Minute 98

Grace and the Law

"For the grace of God has appeared that offers salvation to all people." Titus 2:11

Some avoid reading the Old Testament because they think it is full of "the laws" God gave his people. While this is true, we see from the very beginning of Genesis that God gave grace to individuals who broke the law.

God gave Adam and Eve proper clothing, a lesson in sacrifice, and he sent them out of the garden. He did this so they would not eat of the Tree of Life that would have doomed them to living on this earth forever in bodies that decay. God also gave Cain grace, even after Cain murdered his only brother and rudely reacts to God's words. God was gracious enough to put some kind of mark on Cain, protecting him from others who might seek revenge for the man's deadly actions.

How about a few more examples? God forgave murderers such as Moses, who killed an Egyptian, and David for murdering his lover's husband. God gave Samson strength once again to avenge his eyes and gave Jonah patience and forgiveness. The entire Old Testament is full of grace. Why?

It is the grace of God that leads people to repentance. Are there consequences when we disobey God's laws? Of course, but when God offers grace, because Jesus paid the punishment for sin on the cross, *that* is more powerful than the law.

Perhaps we should show more grace to others around us.

Minute 99

No Other Gods

"One day, after Moses had grown up, he went out to where his own people were and watched them at their hard labor. He saw an Egyptian beating a Hebrew, one of his own people. Looking this way and that and seeing no one, he killed the Egyptian and hid him in the sand." Exodus 2:11-12

I attended Sunday school during my growing-up years. I loved to hear the Bible Stories. I always gave these lessons great thought and there was one consistent thing I wondered about. Why did the people of the Old Testament worship stone images? It seemed silly to me. It wasn't until I was an adult when it occurred to me that there are other types of idols that people worship. This caused me to realize I am guilty of the same

219

sin these biblical characters did I thought was ridiculous.

The very first of the 10 Commandments says to have "no other gods before me." Considering this, I sat back and thought with confidence, *I've got this one!* I discovered, however, the arrogance of this thinking because any time I decide to break one of God's statutes, I have put myself in God's place. I'm saying, "I know better than God."

Moses does this very thing in Exodus 2. He knows God called him to be a deliverer of God's people, who are slaves in Egypt. Knowing this, Moses saw an Egyptian beating an Israelite slave, and he took it upon himself to deliver that Hebrew. He killed the Egyptian, but it didn't go well for Moses. Because he made himself God, Moses had to run for his life and hide for 40 years in the desert.

Could it be the Israelites were slaves for 40 extra years because Moses made this choice? Maybe. Maybe not. What we know is anytime we put ourselves in the place of God, the outcome is never good.

Notes

Minute 100

The Importance of Rest

"Let us, therefore, make every effort to enter that rest, so that no one will perish by following their example of disobedience."
Hebrews 4:11

Spending much of my time with 11- and 12-year-old boys, I can quickly recognize when most of them are restless. They are fidgety, and as a result, they often do things that get them in trouble. The trick is to get them engaged in something productive at the first sign of boredom. I have been successful in drawing the boys into something other than what they were doing, but I have to remind myself that acting restless and needing rest are two different things.

Rest is more than just going to bed; sleeping deeply and awakening refreshed. Rest can also mean to be calm and at peace within yourself. These are equally important, as sleep is to the body.

The first 11 verses of Hebrews have the word rest eleven times. Though the context of these verses concerns God's rest in the next life in heaven with him, the writer of Hebrews was using a word his readers can understand.

We sometimes overlook the importance of rest. Jesus went out alone to rest and God designated the seventh day for it. It is vital that we place a priority on rest. Not taking the time for this detrimentally affects this life and the next one.

Notes:

Other books by Susan Grant:

The Bottle House

Deeply wounded, Stacy Meadows, Stefan Krause and Debbie Young all travel to Bethany R & L Behavior Healthcare Center. As they struggle with individual grief and despair, they meet Chaplain Joseph Miller, who has a mysterious collection of bottles. In time, these three discover that Joseph possesses separate bottles for each of them, whose content is unknown. He labels these bottles, each of various shape, sizes and colors, with their names. As Stacy, Stefan and Debbie work through their grief, Joseph reveals more of the bottles' purposes, culminating in a surprise revelation that restores hope and joy in all three lives.

100 Minutes with God

To be expanded the summer of 2022, similar in length to *Another 100 Minutes with God.*

100 Minutes with God is written for those who struggle with finding time to spend with him. These individual minutes make it possible to connect. with our Creator and provide you with material you can contemplate throughout your day.

Available on Amazon
and other online bookstores.

About the Author

Susan Grant is a graduate of Columbia International University. She taught Bible history in the public schools of North Carolina for eighteen years and was instrumental in growing the program from one full-time teacher to three.

When not writing, Susan now teaches language arts and lives with her husband on the beautiful coast of Maine. Susan enjoys reading, sewing and playing with her dachshund.

You can read more of Susan's writing and sign up for her mailing list at susan-grant.com .

Made in the USA
Las Vegas, NV
16 February 2022

44025484R00125